One Year in Devotional Studies

One Year in Devotional Studies

with Reverend Gregory L. Williamson

Editor
Ray Glandon

Senior Editor
Johnathon Patterson

Senior Publisher
Steven Hill

ASA Publishing Corporation
ASA Publishing Company

A Publisher Trademark Title page

ASA Publishing Corporation
An Accredited Publishing House with the BBB

105 E. Front St., Suite 101
Monroe, Michigan 48161
www.asapublishingcorporation.com

    All Rights Reserved. No part of this publication may be reproduced, stored in a retrieval system or transmitted in any form or by any means electronic, mechanical, photocopying, recording or otherwise, without the prior written permission of the publisher. Author/writer rights to "Freedom of Speech" protected by and with the "1st Amendment" of the Constitution of the United States of America. This is a work of Christian beliefs. Any resemblance to actual events, locales, person living or deceased is entirely coincidental. Other names, places, and characters are within the work of biblical knowledge and its entirety is from the ministerial aspects of its author.

    Any and all vending sales and distribution not permitted without full book cover and this title page.

Copyrights©2016 Reverend Gregory L. Williamson, All Rights Reserved
Book: One Year in Devotional Studies
Date Published: 03.24.16/Edition 1 *Trade Paperback*
Book ASAPCID: 2380685
ISBN: 978-1-886528-35-2
Library of Congress Cataloging-in-Publication Data

        This book was published in the United States of America.
                State of Michigan

A Publisher Trademark Copy page

Dedication of Appreciation

*"I would like to give my
deepest gratitude and appreciation to
my lovely wife, Janice A. Williamson for providing
most of the photographs from our various
recent travel experiences."*

Multiple Bible Versions used
in various scriptural locations:

- *King James Version (KJV)*
- *New King James Version (NKJV)*
- *The Message Bible (TMB)*
- *Easy to Read Version (ERV)*
- *Voice of God Version (VOG)*
- *Amplified Bible (AMP)*
- *New International Version (NIV)*

Table of Contents

One Year in Devotional Studies

Week 1	A New Man Resolution	1
Week 2	Achieving Through Believing	5
Week 3	How Low Can You Go?	9
Week 4	Failing Forward	13
Week 5	Putting God First	17
Week 6	It's All About Love	21
Week 7	Loved More Than We May Know	25
Week 8	Do You Love Me?	29
Week 9	Our Omnipotent Help	33
Week 10	Stay In The Ship	37
Week 11	In His Image	41
Week 12	Stay Connected	45
Week 13	A Matter of Perception	49
Week 14	Wholeheartedness	53
Week 15	Happy and Content	57
Week 16	The Benefits of Doing Good	16

Week 17	Put Your Guard Up	65
Week 18	The Good Fight	69
Week 19	Life's Pharaohs	73
Week 20	Real Power and Strength	77
Week 21	Our Sixth Sense	81
Week 22	Understanding the Times	85
Week 23	Spiritual Identity Theft	89
Week 24	What Are You Thinking?	93
Week 25	God's Rivers of Water	97
Week 26	Whining About Our Dining	101
Week 27	Character	105
Week 28	Discipline Defeats Foolishness	109
Week 29	Family Inheritance	113
Week 30	Passing the Torch	117
Week 31	The Person Behind the Name	121
Week 32	We Are Family	125
Week 33	Illuminating a Dark Day	129
Week 34	Defining Storms	133
Week 35	What Are You Standing On?	137
Week 36	The Presence of "The LORD"	141

Week 37	Wisdom's Response	145
Week 38	A Work Around	149
Week 39	What's Most Important?	153
Week 40	My "Real" Objective	157
Week 41	Fear Not, It Is Written!	161
Week 42	Only By Faith!	165
Week 43	God Changes Things	169
Week 44	Preparation for Running	173
Week 45	As "It" Is Written	177
Week 46	Humbling Ourselves	181
Week 47	Using the Strong Name	185
Week 48	For This I Give You Praise	189
Week 49	How Good Is Your Memory?	193
Week 50	Where Are You?	197
Week 51	They Found Him	201
Week 52	Looking for Opportunities	205

One Year in Devotional Studies

with Reverend Gregory L. Williamson

One Year in Devotional Studies

Week 1

A New Man Resolution

[20] "But ye have not so learned Christ; [21] If so be that ye have heard him, and have been taught by him, as the truth is in Jesus: [22] That ye put off concerning the former conversation the old man, which is corrupt according to the deceitful lusts; [23] And be renewed in the spirit of your mind; [24] And that ye put on the new man, which after God is created in righteousness and true holiness."
Ephesians 4:20-24

Well, we are into a New Year, and if you are like most people, you have probably made some "New Year resolutions." Equally true for most of us is, how long will it take for us to give up on our resolutions: But why is it that we seem to fail more than we succeed in our resolutions? That is a very good question. There are a variety of reasons for failure and success. Commitment, planning, support, focus, realistic expectations and a refusal to quit or give in are the main benefactors to success, and the absence of these can and most often will lead to failure. With that being said, there is a more vital and imperative necessity that should not be overlooked: making sure your resolution properly aligns itself with God's purpose and timing for your life. So how do we do that?

To build anything you must construct it one piece, one layer, one item, or one step at a time. You must have the Blueprint and the instructions. This will provide the best opportunity to produce what the designer had in mind. Too often, things, vehicles, houses, garments, etc. have been put together without the print, drawings, directions, etc. and they are not working as well as intended. So where do I get the print, plans, drawings, etc. for my resolutions? Good question, but you already know the answer: The Bible.

God is more concerned with your "New Man" resolution than He is your "New Year's" resolution. Yes, before we plan, determine and decide what our New Year's resolution is going to be, we must first go to God – (Matthew 6:33) and see what He has planned for our life in 2015. Paul's words throughout the epistle to the Ephesian community is the same message he's conveying to us. He is saying this is where you once were and this is where you are now, IN CHRIST JESUS.

At Ephesians 4:20, Paul says "Ye have not so learn Christ." You have been taught the way of Christ because I have provided you that proper teaching. Therefore, allow the transforming word of God to destroy the old man, old nature, old or former way of thinking (stinkin-thinkin), doing things or changing your circumstances because they really just get worse and worse even though they seem to be better on the outer surface. Be renewed, changed, metamorphosized (Romans 12:1-2) in your heart and mind so that your thinking becomes pleasing to Him and we become the men and women of God He called, purposed, predestined and wants us to be.

A New Year's resolution is a good start for change and good intentions. However, a New Man Resolution is a better choice, and it yields better results. Most and more importantly, it pleases God. Happy New Year! Be Blessed in Jesus Name, Amen.

One Year in Devotional Studies

Daily Devotional Reading

Week 1

- **Monday -** Romans 6:4
- **Tuesday -** 2 Corinthians 5:17
- **Wednesday -** Psalms 40:3
- **Thursday -** 1 Corinthians 15:45
- **Friday -** Psalms 1
- **Saturday –** Revelation 2:17

One Year in Devotional Studies

Week 2

Achieving Through Believing

"I can do all things through Christ which strengtheneth me."
Philippians 4:13

It is truly a blessing to have the faith and confidence that in whatever you go through, you will fully trust and rely on God to see you through it. We must keep in mind that there are trials and temptations that we stumble into and some we get into by planning, striving and conniving, whether we admit it or not. When we fall into these trials, we are told in James 1:2, **to be joyful about it.** "My brethren, count it all joy when ye fall into divers temptations." He goes on to say in verses 3 and 4, "Knowing this, that the trying of your faith worketh patience. But let patience have her perfect work, that ye may be perfect and entire, wanting nothing."

Now, if our struggles are self-created, we should not expect God to provide the spiritual strength to get through those, even though He will still provide us a way out – I Cor. 10:13, "There hath no temptation taken you but such as is common to man: but God is faithful, who will not suffer you to be tempted above that ye are able; but will with the temptation also make a way to escape, that ye may be able to bear it."

Reverend Gregory L. Williamson

When Paul says in verse 13 of Philippians chapter 4, "I can do," this word "do" is translated in the Greek as "Endure." Paul is actually saying, I can endure all things for the cause and sake of Christ. When we are operating in agreement with the will of God, God will always be faithful and just to provide the necessary strength, stamina, courage, fortitude, needed to stand strong while enduring the test.

How do we know when it's us and when it's God? Are we causing our own pain, or is God allowing it to build character? That's a great question, and the answer is found in verse 8, "Finally, brethren, whatsoever things are true, whatsoever things are honest, whatsoever things are just, whatsoever things are pure, whatsoever things are lovely, whatsoever things are of good report; if there be any virtue, and if there be any praise, think on these things."

If we stay on track and stay committed to giving the things of God priority in our lives, we will, like Paul, also experience Successful Achieving derived from our Scriptural Believing. Matthew 6:33 is a great reminder, "But seek ye first the kingdom of God, and his righteousness; and all these things shall be added unto you." My prayer for you in Jesus Name, Amen.

One Year in Devotional Studies

Daily Devotional Reading

Week 2

- **Monday -** St. Matthew 21:22
- **Tuesday -** St. John 20:27
- **Wednesday -** 1 Timothy 6:2
- **Thursday -** 1 Peter 1:8
- **Friday -** 2 Corinthians 5:7
- **Saturday -** 1 Samuel 7:14

One Year in Devotional Studies

WEEK 3

How Low Can You Go?

"Let this mind be in you, which was also in Christ Jesus:"
Philippians 2:6

There used to be a dance program called the "Limbo," and one phrase used constantly as people did the limbo was, "How low can you go?" Well, I'm not talking about that. You may have heard someone occasionally say, "I am about to give up, I am as low as I can go." Well, I'm not talking about that either. What I am focusing on is the lowliness of Humility; although not very popular, it is the most effective means of communicating real love and affection. The whole chapter of Philippians 2 not only speaks to the necessity of humility and how important it is for believers to show love, kindness, tenderness, forgiveness and a lot of other "nesses" toward others – but especially toward other believers. To cement this point, Paul uses our perfect example, "Jesus." Verse 5 says, "Let this mind be in you which was also in Christ Jesus." What mind is that? The one person that had it all, owned it all, deserved it all, created it all yet sacrificed it all and sacrificed it all for us, Jesus. That is humility at its highest. We may not be able to reach the heights that Jesus did, but we can surely show kindness and concern for others with a special focus on other believers. We can

Reverend Gregory L. Williamson

Pray for each other and not Prey on each other. We can choose to think the best about each other in faith, rather than think the worst based on what we see or hear. We walk by Faith, NOT by sight. We can incorporate the principles of a Hezekiah Walker song, "I Need You to Survive." I pray for you and you pray for me because we are all a part of God's family. We need each other. Our Prayers can and will change people and situations when they are focused on the needs of others and the one that hears and answers them – All Mighty God.

I Need You to Survive

I need you, you need me.
We're all a part of God's body.
Stand with me, agree with me.
We're all a part of God's body.

It is his will, that every need be supplied.
You are important to me, I need you to survive.
You are important to me, I need you to survive.

I pray for you, You pray for me.
I love you, I need you to survive.
I won't harm you with words from my mouth.
I love you, I need you to survive.

It is his will, that every need be supplied.
You are important to me, I need you to survive.

One Year in Devotional Studies

Daily Devotional Reading

Week 3

- **Monday -** *Proverbs 15:33*
- **Tuesday -** *Acts 20:19*
- **Wednesday -** *Colossians 2:18*
- **Thursday -** *1 Peter 5:5*
- **Friday -** *Psalms 138:6*
- **Saturday -** *St. Luke 15:16*

One Year in Devotional Studies

Week 4

FAILING FORWARD

³⁶ *"And some days after Paul said unto Barnabas, Let us go again and visit our brethren in every city where we have preached the word of the LORD, and see how they do. ³⁷ And Barnabas determined to take with them John, whose surname was Mark. ³⁸ But Paul thought not good to take him with them, who departed from them from Pamphylia, and went not with them to the work. ³⁹ And the contention was so sharp between them, that they departed asunder one from the other."*

Acts 15:36-39

Who God is, what he has done, and what he has promised to do have been fully documented in scripture. We are often faced with the challenge of deciding whether he is worthy of our trust and if we will choose to exercise trust in him or not. Notice the word *choose.* It comes down to a matter of choice in the end. The earlier generation of Israelites "refused" to trust the Lord. Now the later generation was being given their chance to choose or refuse. We have the same opportunity every day of our lives. When most of us look back over our lives, we had parents and grandparents that had a greater degree of trust and commitment than we exhibit today, or than we exhibit. I often wonder why that is.

It's interesting to see how Mark was restored, how the apostle Paul, who had been so scathing and unwavering in his criticism of him earlier, had been so generous in recognizing the restoration. Moreover, he accepted the fact that God's grace had restored him, and therefore Paul very readily reinstated John Mark as an invaluable servant of Jesus. He recognized grace at work in the life of John Mark. What a tremendous lesson there is in this for us all.

Sometimes I think it is because they had less and because of it, they depended on God for the rest. Sometimes I think it is because we are, far more spoiled that they were. We want to have everything, and we want it right now. Someone mentioned the term "layaway" to me a few days ago. If you don't know what "layaway" is, there was a time a generation or two back where if you wanted something and didn't have all of the money to purchase it, you put it on "layaway" and you paid it down until you paid it off. Then you took it home. I never liked layaway but I remember my parents used it. It's interesting that sometimes before they paid the amount down for the merchandise, they decided they didn't want it and used the money for something else. Maybe layaway is not a bad idea. Maybe it would provide us a little extra time to really think about our decisions before consummating the deal.

But lo and behold, our banking institutions came to our rescue. Because we developed a gotta have it now attitude, they helped us out (we thought) and created "CREDIT CARDS."

The end result is in reverse but the same. Israel's forefathers failed to trust, and the current generation is, being reminded of their failure and the consequences. Our forefathers (parents and grandparents) succeeded where we are failing. We are failing to trust God for what we need, and we are putting our trust in man for what we want.

There will always be times when some of our decisions will be wrong. The true measure of a person is not how often or how many times they fail; it's what happens after. It's how they use

One Year in Devotional Studies

that experience. If it propels a person to better choices in the future, that's failing forward. Either way, we are still left with a choice to make. Will it be God, or will it be man? We either choose to trust, or we refuse to trust. If we choose guidance from any other source besides God through the Holy Spirit, our choice is refuse. And the result? It's living in this land of promise wandering in its wildernesses.

Daily Devotional Reading

Week 4

- **Monday -** *Exodus 14:15*
- **Tuesday -** *St. John 8:10-11*
- **Wednesday -** *St. Matthew 26:75*
- **Thursday -** *Acts 26:14*
- **Friday -** *Psalms 73:26*
- **Saturday -** *Joshua 1:5*

 One Year in Devotional Studies

Week 5

Putting God First

"But seek ye first the kingdom of God, and his righteousness; and all these things shall be added unto you."
St. Matthew 6:33

Considering the routine responsibilities and unexpected challenges that we have to deal with every day, "how do we put or keep God first?" As difficult a question that seem to be, it really isn't. In the Gospel of John, chapter 17:11 (b portion), Jesus says, "Holy Father, keep through thine own name those whom thou hast given me, *that they may be one, as we are*." Matthew 6:32-3 says, "for your heavenly Father knoweth that ye have need of all these things. ³³ But seek ye first the kingdom of God, and his righteousness; and all these things shall be added unto you."

Putting and Keeping God first requires both a relationship with Him and our Trust in Him. Even though we often think we control our relationship with God, that's not true. He creates the relationship. At John 14:6, we find these words, "Jesus saith unto him, I am the way, the truth, and the life: no man cometh unto the Father, but by me.

Reverend Gregory L. Williamson

He draws us unto Himself through various means that uniquely get our attention. I know we sometimes, OK, many times, bring trouble into our lives, but there are times that we do all the right things and trouble still comes. That's when God is allowing a struggle. It might be to strengthen us, or it could be to humble us. When we seek the solution to our problems from and through Him "First", an opportunity for our relationship to strengthen is created. If we patiently observe and reflect on How He has always worked out our challenges, our level of trust and confidence in Him increases. If we don't, well, I don't need to explain what happens. We all have our own stories to tell.

Now before you start to think, "I can't do that", let me assure you that "you already are doing that." It may not be God that you are putting your full trust in, but each one of us has experienced times when we had to deal with something bigger than we are. We each also have a particular *manner* or habitual way of confronting our issues. We might depend on a spouse, friend, neighbor, job, shopping trip, ballgame, etc., but bottom line, we put our full confidence in "that person's or that thing's" ability to make our situation better. God is saying to us at Matthew 6:33 put Him in that place. Come to Me, First, and I will bring balance, focus and priority into your life and add all of the other tangible things you need in your life. That's How You Put God First, and it is very possible to do. May we commit to putting God first in our lives? In Jesus Name, Amen.

One Year in Devotional Studies

Daily Devotional Reading

Week 5

- **Monday -** *Deuteronomy 26:2*
- **Tuesday -** *Nehemiah 8:18*
- **Wednesday -** *Isaiah 44:6*
- **Thursday -** *St. Mark 12:30*
- **Friday -** *Acts 13:46*
- **Saturday -** *Hebrews 5:12*

One Year in Devotional Studies

Week 6

It's All About Love

"And thou shalt love the Lord thy God with all thy heart, and with all thy soul, and with all thy mind, and with all thy strength: this is the first commandment."

St. Mark 12:30

It is interesting that our Lord presented this information as a commandment. You wouldn't think that we would need to be commanded to "love." Nevertheless, I think the message from our Lord is to give God "first" priority in your life with love being the motivation behind it. It is then that you will be on track to the kind of relationship necessary to fulfill His expectation for your life. Always remember that "fulfill" is being "filled" with the "fullness" of Christ. Begin with priority (Matthew 6:33) and add to it Godly love (I Corinthians 13) –

[33] But seek ye first the kingdom of God, and his righteousness; and all these things shall be added unto you.

[1] If I speak with human eloquence and angelic ecstasy but don't love, I'm nothing but the creaking of a rusty gate. [2] If I speak God's Word with power, revealing all his mysteries and making everything plain as day, and if I have faith that says to a mountain,

"Jump," and it jumps, but I don't love, I'm nothing. [3-7] If I give everything I own to the poor and even go to the stake to be burned as a martyr, but I don't love, I've gotten nowhere. So, no matter what I say, what I believe, and what I do, I'm bankrupt without love.

LOVE

Never gives up.
Cares more for others than for self.
Doesn't want what it doesn't have.
Doesn't strut.
Doesn't have a swelled head.
Doesn't force itself on others.
Isn't always "me first."
Doesn't fly off the handle.
Doesn't keep score of the sins of others.
Doesn't revel when others grovel.
Takes pleasure in the flowering of truth.
Puts up with anything.
Trusts God always.
Always looks for the best.
Never looks back.
Keeps going to the end.

For right now, until that completeness, we have three things to do to lead us toward that consummation: Trust steadily in God, hope unswervingly and love extravagantly. We must however, always remember that the best of the three is love. In Jesus Name, Amen.

One Year in Devotional Studies

Daily Devotional Reading

Week 6

- **Monday -** Romans 8:37
- **Tuesday -** St. John 3:16
- **Wednesday -** 1 Samuel 20:17
- **Thursday -** Revelation 1:5
- **Friday -** 1 John 2:9-10
- **Saturday -** St. John 13:34

One Year in Devotional Studies

Week 7

Loved More Than We May Know

"But God commendeth his love toward us, in that, while we were yet sinners, Christ died for us."

Romans 5:8

Roman 5:8 says that God commended His love toward us in that while we were "Yet" or "Still" sinners, Christ dies for us. If we are honest with ourselves, dying or sacrificing for someone who has wronged us or on the outer surface shows no signs of usefulness to us is and would probably always be as far from our thinking as east is from west. I do agree that some would risk their life for a good cause. But even then, there is a difference between risking one's life and intentionally dying for someone. The latter is very, very, very rare. Why did God sacrifice His Son for us? Why did Christ die on our behalf? Other than the fact that He (They) so loved us and still loves us as John 3:16 says, that He gave His only begotten Son, that whosoever believeth in Him should not perish but shall have everlasting life. God showed His love for us while we were sinners but He does not want us to waste that love by staying in sin and becoming comfortable in that sinful state. Allow me to answer the earlier question this way; God didn't sacrifice His Son for who we were. He gave His Son for who we could and would become "IN HIM". That's a good model for us. Let's love others for what they will be and not for who or what they might be at the time. Consider Ephesians 3:19-21

> [19] And to know the love of Christ, which passeth knowledge, that ye might be filled with all the fullness of God.
>
> [20] Now unto him that is able to do exceeding abundantly above all that we ask or think, according to the power that worketh in us,
>
> [21] Unto him be glory in the church by Christ Jesus throughout all ages, world without end. Amen.

ROM 5:6-8 says, you see, at just the RIGHT TIME, when we were still powerless, Christ died for the ungodly. Very rarely will anyone die for a righteous person, though for a good person someone might possibly dare to die. But God demonstrates his own love for us in this: WHILE WE WERE STILL SINNERS, CHRIST DIED FOR US.

Someone accurately shared this with me, 1 cross + 3 nails = 4 given. In Jesus Name, Amen.

One Year in Devotional Studies

Daily Devotional Reading

Week 7

- **Monday -** *Exodus 14:15*
- **Tuesday -** *St. John 8:10-11*
- **Wednesday -** *St. Matthew 26:75*
- **Thursday -** *Acts 26:14*
- **Friday -** *Psalms 73:26*
- **Saturday -** *Joshua 1:5*

One Year in Devotional Studies

Week 8

Do You Love Me?

> After breakfast, Jesus said to Simon Peter, "Simon, son of John, do you love me more than these?" "Yes, Master, you know I love you." Jesus said, "Feed my lambs."
>
> *St. John 21:15*

So a woman said to her Boyfriend/Fiancé of two years, John, do you love me? He replied, "Yes, you know I love you." She then said, "Then Marry Me!" How many times have we heard or uttered these words? Not only are these words common when it comes to relationships and marriage but these words are often deal makers and breakers in so many aspects of our lives.

Responding appropriately to this question requires an accurate assessment and understanding of intent from the one posing the inquiry. Love carries along with it, responsibility, accountability, commitment and sacrifice. How much of it and the categorical proportions vary from situation to situation or relationship to relationship.

In the Gospel of John, chapter 21:15-23, Jesus held a conversation with Peter. He asked him three times, "Do You Love Me?" Peter responded affirmatively all three times yet he never really grasped the magnitude of Jesus' inquiry. So many times, we respond to questions with the answer we perceive the other person wants to hear. That may not be in alignment with what we truthfully think or feel but, "It's just a question, right." More often than not, we discover, after the damage has been done, that we should have given more thought to the question before responding.

The nameless woman at the intro of this discussion may feel that 2 years of dating is long enough to make a decision to marry or not marry. There could obviously be other factors that would explain why this couple is still dating and not married but the point is, she asked a specific question and an immediate response is given without delving into the reason or specific purpose for the question.

As Jesus was about to ascend to His Father and entrust His disciples to continue His work, He knew that a proper, pointed and purposeful Love for God was the only way this mission would be successfully continued and completed. Peter answered consistently in the affirmative but was troubled with the questioning because he knew, as he stated, Lord you know everything. You have to know that I love you. Jesus wanted to emphasize the importance of focus and the progressive challenges that he along with the other disciples would encounter. *Thou wilt keep him in perfect peace, whose mind is stayed on thee: because he trusteth in thee – Isaiah 26:3.* As Jesus reveals to Peter what suffering he will endure, He incudes you will Glorify God in it. Peter's focus is on John, not how he will Glorify God. He asked in verses 21-22, Master, what's going to happen to him? Jesus says to Peter in the following two verses, never mind his assignment, You Follow Me!

If we want to truthfully answer the "love question" with a Yes, we must know what the expectations are. Whether it's dating, marring or our relationship with Jesus, are we willing to be responsible, accountable and committed to "our" assignment. If we are, then we stay focused on that and our actions will answer

 One Year in Devotional Studies

for us; Yes Baby, or Yes Master, you know I love you. I Glorify God by loving you. Love Never Fails! (I Cor. 13) In Jesus Name, Amen.

Daily Devotional Reading

Week 8

- **Monday -** 1 Thessalonians 3:12
- **Tuesday -** Ruth 4:15
- **Wednesday -** 1 Samuel 18:1
- **Thursday -** St. John 21:15-17
- **Friday -** 1 Samuel 1:5
- **Saturday -** 1 John 3:18

One Year in Devotional Studies

Week 9

Our Omnipotent Help

> "Blessed are you, O Israel;
> Who is like you, a people saved by the LORD,
> Who is the shield of your help
> And the sword of your majesty!
> So your enemies will cringe before you,
> And you will tread upon their high places."
> Deuteronomy 33:29

It has been appropriately said that in time of need, one will either encounter people who are willing to help but are unable or people who are able to help but are unwilling. What's rare are times when we find those who are both willing and able to help in time of need.

For the believer in Christ, those encounters only apply to the solutions we seek from human sources. We always have help not only in time of need but also Omnipotent help. The blessedness of Omnipotent help is that it is always able and always willing. WOW, what a position to be in.

God is not only more powerful than any opposition that challenges us, He is Power. That means that the power associated with the seemingly insurmountable challenges we experience, no matter how enormous they may appear, is a subset or a fraction of energy borrowed from God. He is allowing it, but He will bring Glory and Honor to Himself as a result of it.

That's why Moses could exclaim as he does at Deuteronomy 33:29 – How unbelievably blessed we are as saved children of God. The All-Powerful One is our shield of protection. We are protected by His almighty sword. No one can successfully challenge His arsenal. Therefore, those that wrongly oppose us will ultimately cringe in frustration and defeat to their own demise. Those seemingly great fortresses will crumble and disintegrate. And yet, in a way that only God can orchestrate, those monuments will become our testimonies. I heard Dr. Freddy Haynes Jr. say it this way, "God makes your haters, your elevators."

We have the greatest, most powerful source of help there is. His reputation is impeccable. He has never lost a battle. The battle is not ours, it's His. However, we must be patient and let God be God. Every day has 24 hours. Every fight has 12 rounds. Every football game has four quarters. You get the point. A lot goes on in the first half, but in the end, WE WIN! Why? It is because of "Our Omnipotent Help." Be Blessed in the Lord. In Jesus Name, Amen.

One Year in Devotional Studies

Daily Devotional Reading

Week 9

- **Monday -** Psalms 3
- **Tuesday -** 2 Kings 6:27
- **Wednesday -** Psalms 46:1
- **Thursday -** 2 Chronicles 25:8
- **Friday -** Hebrews 13:6
- **Saturday -** Psalms 28:7

One Year in Devotional Studies

Week 10

Stay in The Ship

Paul said to the centurion and to the soldiers, Except these abide in the ship, ye cannot be saved.
Acts 27:31

As travelers plan their vacations, one decision that has to be made is the means of travel. Most of the time, the destination dictates or at least has some bearing on the mode of travel. One area of vacationing that includes the mode of travel is cruising. There are various names and types of boats or ships, but to cruise, you have to travel by ship.

When traveling by ship, you will sometimes encounter challenging weather. Sometimes the challenge is minor, and sometimes it can be life threatening. One precaution cruise lines take is holding a mandatory safety session before the ship leaves the dock. It can be as boring as the demonstration you get on a plane prior to or soon after takeoff. Nevertheless, the safety demo must be conducted, and it is in our best interest to know what to do in the event of an emergency.

In Acts chapter 27, Paul was in route by ship, as a prisoner, to be brought before Caesar. Although winds and storms became severely challenging while in route, Paul was confident that they would make it safely to their destination because God had spoken to him and assured him that he would in fact be brought before Caesar. Paul was confident because not only did he have an intimate relationship with God he had from the inception of his ministry, a personal encounter with Jesus Christ. He says in verse 23 that "The Angel of God" stood by me. The angel of God is no other than Jesus Christ Himself manifested.

As we traverse through life by means of our various ships, we will face challenges that are intended to encourage us to leave the ship. I caution you, that is the influence of the devil. He knows that the ship is the safest place to be and that all those in the ship will be saved. If he can entice you to leave the ship, he stands a better chance at derailing you. The ship that I am speaking of, however, has nothing to do with boards, planks, rafts, lifeboats or any other items like those. I am speaking of "Relation 'ship'."

If you stay in your relationship with Christ, you will find safety and refuge unlike no other. Staying in relationship with Christ creates "Fellowship," which leads to "Discipleship" which develops "stewardship," and ultimately establishes a friendship through the partnership of ownership, that assures your membership in the paradise Heaven that God has prepared for us. If you are in relationship with Christ, you will come to know His voice, His desire and His purpose for your life, but you must remain in the ship. The best advice is just what Paul advised his acquaintances to do, "Stay in the Ship." In Jesus Name, Amen.

One Year in Devotional Studies

Daily Devotional Reading

Week 10

- **Monday -** Acts 27:31
- **Tuesday -** 1 Corinthians 1:9
- **Wednesday -** 1 John 1:6
- **Thursday -** 2 Corinthians 6:14
- **Friday -** Acts 2:42
- **Saturday -** Exodus 33:11

One Year in Devotional Studies

Week 11

In His Image

"So God created man in his own image, in the image of God created he him; male and female created he them."
Genesis 1:27

I'm not sure if we can see ourselves as God does, but if we focus on the principles that God reveals in His word when we consider ourselves, we should walk with our head up, shoulders back, and with a little swag. Genesis 1:27 should certainly send the reader a very powerful message. Man is the only part of God's creation that was made in the image of God. That doesn't mean that man is a visual copy that looks like God. It also doesn't mean that man is a god with the same creative abilities that God possesses.

The image of God has to do with the personal and intimate involvement God had in creating Man. Man's creation was a more immediate act of divine wisdom and power than that of the other creatures. Up to the creation of man, the process was, "Let there be light," and "Let there be a firmament," and "Let the earth, or waters, bring forth" such a thing; but now the word of command is turned into a word of consultation, *"Let us make man,* for whose sake the rest of the creatures were made: this is a work we must take into our own hands."

Reverend Gregory L. Williamson

Everything made prior to man was accomplished by the authoritative word of God. However, when we come to the creation of man, God speaks as one having and expressing compassion, affection and delight. Proverbs 8:30 and 31 says, "Then I was by him, as one brought up with him: and I was daily his delight, rejoicing always before him; Rejoicing in the habitable part of his earth; and my delights were with the sons of men."

Being created in the image of God is nothing to be taken lightly. That doesn't mean we should be arrogant or big headed, but we should walk in our God given authority. Romans 12:3 does not tell us not to think highly of ourselves; it says not to think more highly of ourselves than we ought to. How highly ought we to think? Peter says we are "chosen," "royal," and "holy." Walk in that light. Some people may see you as peculiar, but that's OK. Peter says we are to show forth our praises to God because He called us out of darkness into His guiding light. When we don't see ourselves this way, the opposite takes possession of us. We exchange the royal and holy life that makes us peculiar to the world for a life that operates in darkness and eventually becomes weird, strange and unfulfilling. How do you see yourself? I hope you see yourself as the fearfully and wonderfully made person (Psalms 139:14) that God created you to be. Live each day reflecting His image. In Jesus Name, Amen.

One Year in Devotional Studies

Daily Devotional Reading

Week 11

- **Monday -** *Deuteronomy 4:23*
- **Tuesday -** *Genesis 1:27*
- **Wednesday -** *Daniel 3:16-18*
- **Thursday -** *Romans 1:23*
- **Friday -** *2 Corinthians 4:4*
- **Saturday -** *1 Corinthians 13:12*

One Year in Devotional Studies

Week 12

Stay Connected

"I am the true vine, and my Father is the Gardener. He cuts off every branch in me that bears no fruit, while every branch that does bear fruit HE PRUNES so that it will be even more fruitful."
St. John 15:1-2

The verses referenced above represent what this topic focusses on. Verse 5, (not listed above but should be read) provides the why. Jesus states, "I am the vine, ye are the branches: He that abideth in me, and I in him, the same bringeth forth much fruit: for without me ye can do nothing." The "C" portion of that verse makes a strong statement. Jesus says, "Without Me, you can do nothing." Nothing really means nothing, not a thing. If this is true, I am just spinning my wheels when I'm not connected to Jesus in my decision making. So how do I stay connected?

For the Christian, Jesus is not just speaking of spiritual things. He means just what He says, "we can do nothing." Now you may be thinking that you have done many things on various occasions without consulting God through His word and/or prayer. You are right. I have too. However, what Jesus is saying here is that we can do nothing of any significant value, nothing in agreement with His will, nothing that would benefit us as much if we sought Him beforehand.

Reverend Gregory L. Williamson

Since Jesus used a vine to illustrate His point, let's look at what a vine does for the things connected to it. No matter how close or how far a branch or vine is from the root, trunk, or stem of a bush, it will draw nourishment from the source. But the minute it is cut, severed or separated from the bush or "source" if you will, it will slowly begin to dehydrate, wither, and eventually die. That same idea is true with us as well. Sometimes it seems like we're not connected, and we may even think we are not connected to God, but we can't rely on our feelings and thoughts. WE ARE STILL CONNECTED!

I discovered this when I planted a garden for the first time. Some plants took off rather quickly, some a little slower, and some seemed to take forever to push through the dirt. That's when God revealed a correlation that I will always remember. He said some plants require deeper roots to sustain their purpose. He said there is a lot of activity going on beneath the surface sometimes that is not seen above the ground. Even when you think the seeds are not growing, they are. It's the same way with Christians. Even when we think we or others are not growing, trust me, we are growing *because we are connected to the Living Water, Jesus Christ. Stay connected and grow in Grace. In Jesus Name, Amen.*

 One Year in Devotional Studies

Daily Devotional Reading

Week 12

- **Monday -** Mark 3:10
- **Tuesday -** Hebrews 4:15
- **Wednesday -** Ephesians 4:3
- **Thursday -** Psalms 133:1
- **Friday -** 2 Corinthians 6:16
- **Saturday -** Genesis 34:16

One Year in Devotional Studies

Week 13

A Matter of Perception

"When Jesus therefore had received the vinegar, he said, It is finished: and he bowed his head, and gave up the ghost."

St. John 19:30

Whether you refer to it as Easter, Resurrection Day or some other title, this celebrated weekend is everything to followers of Christ. It's what our entire hope is built on. Jesus was God in the flesh. He lived among mankind teaching, healing and being our example.

On that Friday that we call "Good Friday," He settled and paid in full our sin debt. He was arrested, falsely accused, and charged with a crime He didn't commit. He should never have been charged with blasphemy. He was brutally beaten, whipped, scourged, ridiculed, spat on, and then nailed to a cross between two thieves. It was there that He eventually gave up the ghost and died. So why do we call this "Good Friday"?

The bible says the earth reeled and rocked, the ground seemed to split, and there was great darkness, the veil of the temple split in two. We reflect on the 7 sayings Jesus made while on the cross. Then all of a sudden, "It's Over!" It Is Finished! That's the way it seemed because the disciples went home. It's over, they thought. The disciples had a perspective on how Jesus was going to reestablish His kingdom, and it didn't seem to work. They spent Saturday congregated in fear. They didn't know what to expect.

We know that early Sunday morning the tomb was found empty. That changed everything. After finding an empty tomb, encountering a resurrected Savior, and witnessing His ascension, the disciples were restored, renewed and re-energized for service. So why did they have the highs and lows? Part of it was because they did not have the aiding of the Holy Spirit as we do. They did not have the right understanding of what Jesus meant by Establishing His Earthly kingdom. Now it all was beginning to make sense.

Yes, it was a Good Friday, and not because of what they did to Jesus. It was a Good Friday because of what Jesus did for us. Our relationship with God, through Jesus Christ, was restored. Satan's threat of death was defeated. Mankind's destiny took a huge turn for the better.

Now that we have the Holy Spirit as our teacher, comforter and guide, are our actions any different from the disciples? The disciples got caught up in Saturday. Some of us do as well. Jesus' death on the cross paid our sin debt. Jesus rising from the tomb/grave is our victory. Saturday is our challenge. If we sit in sorrow, feeling defeated in our journey, we are living in that Saturday mentality. There are going to be dark days and bright days in our journey. Satan will see to that. Our perspective must be on remembering the price Christ paid on Good Friday while focusing on the great opportunity He gifted us on that Resurrection Sunday. In Jesus Name, Amen.

One Year in Devotional Studies

Daily Devotional Reading

Week 13

- **Monday -** *Judges 6:22*
- **Tuesday -** *Genesis 19:35*
- **Wednesday -** *2 Kings 4:9*
- **Thursday -** *Job 38:18*
- **Friday -** *St. Matthew 13:14*
- **Saturday -** *St. Mark 8:17*

One Year in Devotional Studies

Week 14

Wholeheartedness

"The LORD was furious with Israel and made them wander in the wilderness for forty years until the whole generation that sinned against him had died. But here you are, a brood of sinners, doing exactly the same thing! You are making the LORD even angrier with Israel. If you turn away from him like this and he abandons them again in the wilderness, you will be responsible for destroying this entire nation!"

Numbers 32:13-15

Finally, the children of Israel were about to enter the Promised Land. The time had come to show that they believed God and were committed to his purposes. They would cross the Jordan, overcome the inhabitants, and divide up the land as it was apportioned to them. Then they would receive their inheritance. No time now for uncertainty. It was time for wholehearted commitment!

When the tribes of Reuben and Gad asked if they might be allowed to settle east of Jordan, Moses' reaction was violent! He chided them for their apparent lack of commitment; he analogized their attitude to that of the previous generation, which had chosen not to cross the Jordan, thus resulting in forty years in the wilderness; and he accused them of destroying the morale of the people and jeopardizing the whole venture. Then he pointedly remarked that, of the whole previous generation, only Joshua and Caleb would enter the land, because "they have wholeheartedly followed the Lord" (32:12).

I can relate to Moses' anger over Reuben and Gad's apparent lack of commitment. I am also angered when I look at the devastating results of our culture due to that same kind of lack of commitment. Rather than sacrifice now for a healthier future, too many want it all right now, even if it creates enormous challenges for divorced wives and husbands, single-parented children, and whatever issues that result or fail to develop in same –sex marriages.

Many couples stand before a magistrate of some type to declare and profess their love, commitment and devotion to each other. The alarming divorce rate reveals that those vows are not honored very long. Equally alarming, the divorce rate for Christians is the same as for non-Christians. The overwhelming joy felt and commitment shown by fathers in the delivery room when their sons and/or daughters are born soon fade for many as is indicated by the huge percentages of single-parent households.

This is the time for modern-day Calebs and Joshuas to step forward and show the way, the way to strengthen the knees of the feeble and to lead the uncertain away from the broad paths of compromise into the narrow lanes of commitment. Remember God's command at Joshua 1:5-8. Today, more than ever, is a time for wholehearted commitment. Stay focused on the promises of God. He will never fail us. In Jesus Name, Amen.

One Year in Devotional Studies

Daily Devotional Reading

Week 14

- **Monday -** *Genesis 39:22*
- **Tuesday -** *Joshua 22:16*
- **Wednesday -** *Jeremiah 44:3*
- **Thursday -** *St. Matthew 5:38*
- **Friday -** *Ezekiel 18:28*
- **Saturday -** *St. James 5:15*

One Year in Devotional Studies

Week 15

Happy and Content

¹¹ *"Not that I speak in respect of want: for I have learned, in whatsoever state I am, therewith to be content. ¹² I know both how to be abased, and I know how to abound: everywhere and in all things I am instructed both to be full and to be hungry, both to abound and to suffer need."*

Philippians 4:11-12

There is no truer statement than "If you have Christ, you have everything." The challenge is this: there are so many believers that have Christ, yet so few of those believers realize what that really provides them. If you don't know what you have in your hands, it may be because your hands are closed. God gives to us so that we may give to others. If your hands are open, you can see what you have to share. If your hands are closed, you can't. When we live in poverty, it's not always God's desire that we live that way.

Sometimes it is our inability to open our hands, hearts and/or minds to the understanding of what God wants to impart unto us that we fail to see the fruitfulness and abundance that we have in Him. The recipe is simple – If we want more, we must give more. More of what? More of what He has already given us, and that requires a relationship and commitment to cultivate through study

Reverend Gregory L. Williamson

time, meditation time and listening time. Believe me when I say, we have more than we realize, regardless of what shows on the outside.

The Apostle Paul reminds us at II Cor. 9:15, "Thanks be unto God for his unspeakable gift." The unspeakable gift he is referring to is none other than Jesus Christ, who is indeed the unspeakable gift of God unto this world, a gift we have all reason to be very thankful. We also find these encouraging words at I Peter 4:10, "As every man hath received the gift, even so minister the same one to another, as good stewards of the manifold grace of God." Literally, God has shown us his grace in many different ways. We should be good servants and use whatever gift he has given us in a way that will best serve each other. May we find Joy and contentment in doing just that. I Pray in Jesus Name, Amen.

One Year in Devotional Studies

Daily Devotional Reading

Week 15

- **Monday -** *Genesis 37:27*
- **Tuesday -** *Judges 17:11*
- **Wednesday -** *St. Mark 15:15*
- **Thursday -** *Philippians 4:11*
- **Friday -** *Hebrews 13:5*
- **Saturday -** *Leviticus 10:20*

One Year in Devotional Studies

Week 16

The Benefits of Doing Good

"As we have therefore opportunity, let us do good unto all men, especially unto them who are of the household of faith."

Galatians 6:10

Growing up in a Christian home has its advantages, but at times it can seem very restrictive. I say that with a little bit of humor because in reality, there is no comparison to the advantage of being raised in the knowledge and understanding of God's word. There were times when I couldn't do some of the things my friends could. There were consequences I endured when I did test the waters that I knew I should have stayed clear. Today, I can see the benefits of staying away from the things I did and the consequences from the things I didn't. They also align themselves with Paul's words in Galatians chapter 6, "Whatsoever a man soweth, that shall he also reap." We live off of crops we harvest from the seeds we plant. Our mode of operation is depicted by the way we operate. We are not who we are because of what we do. We do what we do because of who we are. So why do good, and what does it benefit?

Paul admonishes us in this chapter to always be of help to one another and to never stop doing good. He adds, "an especially those of the household of faith," or our fellow believers. My

Reverend Gregory L. Williamson

earthly father, who ironically passed away 23 years ago today, was one of 3 or 4 church trustee/deacons that used their homes as collateral to acquire the additional funding needed to complete the construction of our church building. What was their motivation? Was it because they wanted special recognition? Was it an investment that they later received huge returns on? Did the contributions afford them majority control over future church decisions? Were their names etched in brick and mortar and strategically placed in the building's structure? The answer to all of these questions is, "NO". Sometimes I wonder how my mother agreed to this while risking shelter for 8 children.

What I want to point out is not "what" my father and these three or four men did. It's that they focused on doing something "good" and that there were long term benefits yielded. That church still stands today. This happened in the late 1960s. So think about the number of believers over the years that were led to Christ through that ministry. If you were one that gave your life to Christ in that post construction period, where might you be today had it not been completed? What if that church had become an "eyesore" in the community and people said there used to be a church group here that decided to build, but they never finished.

Doing good does not just impact our immediate situation, it also has "the domino effect." Not only does it affect those around us, it also becomes effective and infectious. It influences, it encourages, it motivates, and it's contagious. I think Paul is just simply saying, in addition to the host of reasons for doing good, "Doing good is just the right thing to do." Doing good puts in motion a positive stimulus that positively impacts everything it touches. Is that not what our Lord and Savior did? During His earthly ministry, He healed, He encouraged, He cried, He taught, He touched, He confronted, He loved, and after fulfilling His purpose, He Restored when He died and rose from the grave for you and me. There is no greater good that could be done than that. "His good" will continue to impact and change mankind until

One Year in Devotional Studies

He returns. I leave you with Psalms 103:2, "Bless the Lord, O my soul, and forget not ALL His Benefits." In Jesus Name, Amen.

Daily Devotional Reading

Week 16

- **Monday -** Galatians 6:9-10
- **Tuesday -** Jeremiah 18:11
- **Wednesday -** Acts 10:38
- **Thursday -** 1 Peter 2:15
- **Friday -** 2 Thessalonians 3:13
- **Saturday -** Titus 2:7

One Year in Devotional Studies

Week 17

Put Your Guard Up

11 "Put on the whole armor of God, which ye may be able to stand against the wiles of the devil."
Ephesians 6:7

A common phrase used to alert someone of a potential threat is "Put your guard up." In consideration of the threat and the one being exposed to it, an attempt to apply the proper guard would begin. Sometimes it might be to fortify yourself, and other times it might be to, simply run for cover. The scripture referenced above warns us that we must guard ourselves against the wiles of Satan. We are warned that we wrestle not against flesh and blood, but against principalities, against powers, against the rulers of the darkness of this world, against spiritual wickedness in high places. Thanks be to God, the verse doesn't end there. Jesus says "But", I am here to provide abundant life.

The contrast of Jesus' purpose compared to that of Satan's is a no brainer. Jesus gives life and Satan tries to destroy it. Even though Satan uses those who are willing to be used to cause this destruction in our lives, God is always in control. Sometimes you will defeat the attempts of Satan by others and sometimes you will fall prey. We are, however, re-equipped for service, through the powerful word of God. It's fascinating how God corrects and provides the required changes all in one swipe.

Whenever God instructs us NOT do something, He immediately follows it up with what we SHOULD do. For example, at Rom 12:2, Paul says, "And be not conformed to this world: but be ye transformed by the renewing of your mind." At Eph. 4:25 and 28 Paul says, "Wherefore putting away lying, speak every man truth with his neighbor and let him that stole steal no more: but rather let him labour, working with his hands the thing which is good."

Whether we experience a successful or unsuccessful encounter with Satan, we are still victors. If we defeat him, it is by the power of the Holy Spirit. If we fall prey, we are strengthened, enlightened and matured through the power of that same Holy Spirit. Sometimes we need to develop in areas that only a challenge or fall can accomplish. Nevertheless, keep in mind, failing doesn't make us a failure. Some people need to be weeded from our lives, and some are planted to assist in our growth and development. Always remember the entire verse, "*A thief is only there to steal and kill and destroy. I came so they can have real and eternal life, more and better life than they ever dreamed of.*" In Jesus Name, Amen

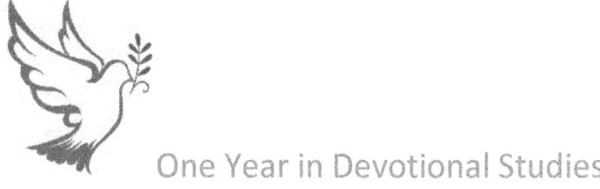

One Year in Devotional Studies

Daily Devotional Reading

Week 17

- **Monday -** *Proverbs 4:23*
- **Tuesday -** *St. Matthew 4:7-11*
- **Wednesday -** *1 Samuel 2:9*
- **Thursday -** *Psalms 39:1*
- **Friday -** *Proverbs 13:6*
- **Saturday -** *Psalms 127:1*

One Year in Devotional Studies

Week 18

The Good Fight

"I have fought the good fight. I have finished the race. I have served the Lord faithfully."
                                                II Timothy 4:7

Fighting is common in our society. Not just in today's environment but all throughout history we can find times where one nation was fighting against another. In the continent of Africa, one tribe fights against another. Within our prison walls, one gang is constantly at war with another. In our schools, one group fights against another. Sadly, fighting even occurs within many church families. The Bible is replete with depictions of quarrels within families, groups, and nations.

In II Timothy, Paul talks about fighting the good fight. Is there such a thing as a good fight? If there is, what exactly is it? Certainly, if there is an attack against you, you have the right to defend and protect yourself. That would be a good fight. If a burglar attempts a break in as a and you're home, you have the right to protect yourself, your family and your property. That's a good fight. Fighting, however, just for the sake of fighting and without a real point or purpose is just a dangerous and many times worthless exercise in futility. Nothing productive is gained unfortunately, many lives can be lost as a result. So what is Paul referencing when he talks about the good fight?

First of all, he is focusing on the Christian Fight. Fighting the Christian fight is an unfair fight because we don't know the number of rounds. But, it is a fixed fight because we always win. In fact we have already won; our victory is in Christ's victory. Paul did not fight out of fear, frustration or confusion because he had the assurance that by the grace of God he was living out his life in the will of God. As a Christian, as a minister, he had fought a good fight. He had gone through the difficulties of his warfare and had gained victory over the powers of darkness. It was a good fight because the cause was good and the victory certain because he was faithful. Even at a difficult time while nearing the end of his life, he could look back on his life and see a trail of "good fighting."

Jesus forewarned us at John 16:33 when He said, "I have told you these things so that you can have peace in me. In this world you will have troubles. But be brave! I have defeated the world!" We must fight this good fight as well. We must fight it out and finish our course. We must not give over till we are made more than conquerors through him who hath loved us. That provides unspeakable comfort. If we stay cognizant of these facts, by the grace of God, we will have fought the "Good Fight" and will finish our course in life with unspeakable joy. In Jesus Name, Amen.

One Year in Devotional Studies

Daily Devotional Reading

Week 18

- **Monday -** 2 Timothy 4:7
- **Tuesday -** Exodus 14:14
- **Wednesday -** 1 Samuel 8:20
- **Thursday -** Nehemiah 4:20
- **Friday -** Psalms 35:1
- **Saturday -** 1 Samuel 17:32

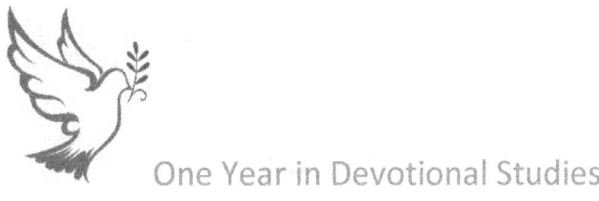

One Year in Devotional Studies

Week 19

Life's Pharaohs

"And the LORD said unto Moses, Pharaoh's heart is hardened, he refuseth to let the people go."

Exodus 7:14

The name "Pharaoh" is not a person; it is a title. Pharaoh was the title given to ancient Egyptian kings. This king was not a man with a "hard" heart. He was a man that God chose to use as a means to show His power as He began the process of freeing Israel from Egypt. At Deuteronomy 2:30b, Moses records, "for the Lord thy God hardened his spirit, and made his heart obstinate, that he might deliver him into thy hand, as appeareth this day." When we read that God hardened Pharaoh's heart, Moses is not implying that God overpowered Pharaoh and forced him to do something that he didn't want to do. God created conditions that forced Pharaoh to make some decisions. Verses 4 and 5 below of Exodus 7 convey why God did what He did.

⁴ But Pharaoh shall not hearken unto you, *that I may lay my hand upon Egypt, and bring forth mine armies, and my people the children of Israel, out of the land of Egypt by great judgments.*

Reverend Gregory L. Williamson

[5] And *the Egyptians shall know that I am the* LORD, when I stretch forth mine hand upon Egypt, and bring out the children of Israel from among them.

Pharaoh had a choice to make. He could realize that he was dealing with omnipotent power and his best course of action would be to submit, or he could operate out of pride and refuse to submit. He chose pride. Sometimes we encounter these same types of decisions. We find ourselves challenged by Pharaohs, and sometimes we are the Pharaohs. What decision do we make?

If you are experiencing challenges in your life (that *you are not causing*), and they don't seem to go away, it just may be that God has hardened the heart of that person or institution that's wreaking havoc in your life. Apply the scriptural principle above and watch God free you from every obstacle that confronts you. God will not force us to do what He desires (like puppets) but He loves us so much that He will continue to oppose our course of travel until we either surrender unto Him or get stuck in a rut.

Jesus told Saul, "It's hard to kick against the prick." He was simply telling Paul that you can't win when you fight against God. Whenever you find yourself going against God's will, let go and let God. Your breakthrough is nearer than you may think. In Jesus Name, Amen.

One Year in Devotional Studies

Daily Devotional Reading

Week 19

- **Monday -** *Genesis 12:17*
- **Tuesday -** *Romans 13:1-3*
- **Wednesday -** *Exodus 6:1*
- **Thursday -** *Ester 9:3*
- **Friday -** *Ephesians 6:12*
- **Saturday -** *Hebrews 11:24*

One Year in Devotional Studies

Week 20

Real Power and Strength!

"He giveth power to the faint; and to them that have no might he increaseth strength."

Isaiah 40:29

One of the greatest building blocks for a believer is the faith maturity process. All believers began the journey of faith with some amount of fear and or doubt. Most have gone through challenges and difficulties that you just knew were going to destroy you and then you begin to see God moving in that struggle. When we make plans and don't consult God first, we plan based on our ability. We must never forget that our strength has and always will be in the power of the Lord. The amount of power we possess does not depend on God's strength but on the amount of our commitment to Him in and through His word.

The power is in His word. The apostle Paul said in II Cor. 12:10

> *"Therefore I take pleasure in infirmities, in reproaches, in necessities, in persecutions, in distresses for Christ's sake: for when I am weak, then am I strong."*

Paul also said at Philippians 4:13, "I can do all things through Christ which strengtheneth me."

Once we align or allow God to align our lives with His will, Satan moves into action. He can and most often will be very annoying. That being said, he cannot win. He cannot defeat you. We must again realize that defeating Satan will not be accomplished in our strength but through the Power of the Holy Spirit. The key to this power is found in God's word. Once we tap in, we become more powerful and dangerous than we can imagine. We can do all things that are in alignment with God's will, and we can endure all things that He has anointed to be a part of our struggle and development.

When we develop the ability to focus on the Glory that God will receive from our successful endurance of any and all devilish attacks of Satan, Satan himself will see the futility in fighting against us because he realizes he's fighting against God. Don't think for a minute he's done. He will refortify his attack weapons but he will return.

Our assurance is in knowing that God is always protecting us from the things we can't handle and equipping us for the things He wants us to handle. Remember Isaiah's words from the reference scripture at Isaiah 40:29 (AMP), "He gives power to the faint *and* weary, and to him who has no might He increases strength [causing it to multiply and making it to abound]." With the strength of God, we can abound in Him. In Jesus Name, Amen.

One Year in Devotional Studies

Daily Devotional Reading

Week 20

- **Monday -** 1 Corinthians 4:20
- **Tuesday -** 2 Samuel 22:33
- **Wednesday -** Nehemiah 1:10
- **Thursday -** Isaiah 40:29
- **Friday -** Job 36:19
- **Saturday -** Psalms 27:1

One Year in Devotional Studies

Week 21

Our Sixth Sense

"For we walk by faith, not by sight:"
II Corinthians 5:7

Unless some circumstance in life have compromised one of your five senses, you have the ability to see, hear, smell, taste and touch. God gives us these abilities to develop ourselves and aid others in life development. Psalms 139:14 talks about how fearfully and wonderfully God made us. These five senses assist us in so many marvelous ways.

The benefit of sight needs no explanation. Witnessing the change of colors in the fall is priceless. Waking up to the sound of birds singing in the morning can be beautiful. The delightful smell of a meal coming from the kitchen can test your patience. Our taste buds work in conjunction with our sense of smell. Lastly, our ability to feel works for us in two ways: we can feel as it relates to touching and feeling, but we also can bear each other's burdens by showing our feelings and letting others know that we care and are concerned.

Even with all of the benefits listed above, our five senses do not and can not assure us that our course in life will be on track and successful. We can only go or grow so far if these five senses alone are utilized. To fully develop into the person that God intends you to be, you must initiate a "sixth sense." That sixth sense is "faith." It is not just faith but faith in God. Faith in anything other than God is faith in one of these other five senses. By this I mean – you will navigate your course of life based on what you see or what you hear, etc. Until we yield our lives to Christ, these five senses are all we have to lead us.

If our heart is properly motivated, we may not do too badly. However, once we accept Christ as Savior and submit to His guidance, our lives are opened to a vast world that is beyond our comprehension. What does that do? It elevates our thinking – (Romans 12:2. When others say there is no growth, they are speaking to a lack of physical change visible to the eye. For the Believer, he knows that sometimes God is growing us inward, sometimes downward, and sometimes outward but always growing us. That's what Paul means (II Cor. 5:7) when he says that we walk by "faith," not by sight. Faith is the sixth sense, and by faith all things and people are in a continuous growth cycle. Our growth cycle includes "Go," "Slow," "Woe," and even "No," but in all of these cycles there is still growth. May we continue to grow In Jesus Name, Amen?

One Year in Devotional Studies

Daily Devotional Reading

Week 21

- **Monday -** Hebrews 5:14
- **Tuesday -** Genesis 1:31
- **Wednesday -** Nehemiah 8:8
- **Thursday -** Malachi 3:18
- **Friday -** Genesis 27:23
- **Saturday -** Ezekiel 44:23

One Year in Devotional Studies

Week 22

Understanding the Times

³² "From the family of Issachar there were 200 wise leaders. These men understood the right thing for Israel to do at the right time. Their relatives were with them and under their command."

I Chronicles 12:32

If it hasn't happened already, you will undoubtedly encounter at least one challenge in life that will require great courage and tenacity. These challenges will often test the very fiber of your being. Yes, Satan will test you to see what you are made of. Vince Lombardi said, "It doesn't matter how many times you get knocked down but how many times you get up." I fully understand his point. As long as you find the strength to get up after each knock down, you're good – Right! The challenge however, is maintaining that *mentality that I can get back up.*

When you attempt that effort on just your own strength and knowledge, it will soon end in failure. This does not mean that you are a failure, but it does mean that your effort failed. We must realize that we are destined to come against obstacles that are larger than we are. We are not equipped to handle them alone. In fact, God does not want us to take them on by ourselves. The power and purpose of God provides for us through the partnering of His Holy Spirit. God will sometimes reveal to us the best way to fix a situation. He may do it through us or through others but either way, it is God's power, not ours, that resolves the problem. We are simply the vehicles He uses to make things happen.

In the reference scripture above, we embark upon a period in Israel's history where King Saul is on his way out and King David is on his way in. The preceding verses of scripture lists the numbers of soldiers that are coming and/or have arrived to support David's Kingship to "protect and defend" him in the event of trouble created by supporters of Saul. All of these verses reflect emotional and physical support, which is good to have. Nevertheless, in times of great challenge and unpredictable outcomes, you want more than physical and emotional support. You want the power and presence of God supporting you, too.

In verse 32, we see that the smallest group that came is recognized as the wisest group of leaders. The passage says that they understood the times, the right thing for Israel to do, and the right time to do it. Equally important, their followers were in total agreement and submitted to their leadership. Following God fearing leaders is invaluable. After all, God appoints them for His purpose.

It's great to have a mighty army to support your conquest, but a great army with a poor strategy or lack of commitment can be, and most often is, a recipe for disaster. Daniel also recognized that God was the only reliable resource for discerning the times. At Daniel 2:20-22, "Daniel answered and said, Blessed be the name of God for ever and ever: for wisdom and might are his: And he changeth the times and the seasons: he removeth kings, and setteth up kings: he giveth wisdom unto the wise, and knowledge to them that know understanding: He revealeth the deep and secret things: he knoweth what is in the darkness, and the light dwelleth with him." **May God bless us to be wise and discerning as Daniel and**

One Year in Devotional Studies

the children of Issachar who spiritually understood the times in which they lived. In Jesus Name, Amen.

Daily Devotional Reading

Week 22

- **Monday -** Malachi 4:4-6
- **Tuesday -** Genesis 41:33-39
- **Wednesday -** 1 Kings 3:11
- **Thursday -** 1 Corinthians 2:14
- **Friday -** Ecclesiastes 8:5
- **Saturday -** 1 Corinthians 11:29

One Year in Devotional Studies

Week 23

Spiritual Identity Theft

"The thief cometh not, but for to steal, and to kill, and to destroy: I am come that they might have life, and that they might have it more abundantly."

St. John 10:10

One of the most unnerving experiences you can encounter in life is becoming a victim of "identity theft." In most cases, when the individual discovers that someone has stolen their credentials and are using their identity, there are layers of damage. By this I mean every time you think your identity has been cleared, just like peeling back a layer of skin from an onion, more damage is discovered. There are so many sophisticated systems of technology available today that you can't be too careful. In fact, it would be advisable for all of us to invest some time researching or attending various seminars on this topic to better understand how we can protect ourselves from these predators.

While I believe that is good advice, protecting our Spiritual Identity is even more important. There is an even more vicious predator seeking tirelessly to steal our "Spiritual Identity." It's no secret who he is. He is none other than Satan. He's on the job 24/7 and has countless numbers of people he has deceived into assisting him in this effort. Many of them appear to be angels of light, but in reality, they, just like their father, are only interested in stealing, killing and destroying the spiritual identity of God's followers. How does he do this?

First of all, Satan knows that he doesn't stand a chance against God. However, he can attack us. When he does, this is his way of getting back at God. He primarily does this by severing relationships. He knows I John 4:4 - …. Greater is He …., he knows Phil. 4:13 – I can do all things …, he knows Rom. 8:31 - …. Who can be successful against us? He knows Gen. 18:14 – Is anything too hard for God? What I am saying here is that Satan knows the word of God. Unfortunately, he knows it better that many of God's followers. Our power is in our relationship with God through His word. We spend too much time focusing on who we think we are instead of who God says we are, who God says we can be, who He desires us to be and who He needs us to be at a particular time in our lives. If we get stuck in one place because we like that spot, we resist God's attempts to move us. God uses various situations and people to move us to the next level. Not just to move us. Not just to make us uncomfortable. He allows these experiences to prepare us for where He is leading us. As I have said many times before, God provides where He guides. When we choose our own direction, we get our self-created results. If we are not nurturing our relationship with Him, we may miss the guidance of His Spirit.

Satan likes it when we allow our personal desires to break our communication with God. That's what happened to Adam in the very beginning. God gave him a responsibility, but he neglected to cherish it and be what he was supposed to be in relationship with God and Eve. Moses focused on his inability to speak fluently instead of on God who created Speech and speaking. God called Gideon a "Mighty Man of Valor" while he was hiding in fear of his death. God sees us for who we were created to be, not where we

One Year in Devotional Studies

are at a particular time in our life. Someone (I don't remember who) once said, "it's not what you are called, it's what you answer to." I pray we stay in close relationship with God through His Holy Spirit so that we not only recognize His call but also fulfill the calling once we acknowledge it. In Jesus Name, Amen.

Daily Devotional Reading

Week 23

- **Monday -** *Genesis 45:1-4*
- **Tuesday -** *1 John 4:1*
- **Wednesday -** *Romans 8:6*
- **Thursday -** *1 Corinthians 2:13*
- **Friday -** *Ephesians 1:3*
- **Saturday -** *1 Corinthians 12:1*

One Year in Devotional Studies

Week 24

What Are You Thinking?

"Finally, brethren, whatsoever things are true, whatsoever things are honest, whatsoever things are just, whatsoever things are pure, whatsoever things are lovely, whatsoever things are of good report; if there be any virtue, and if there be any praise, think on these things."
Philippians 4:8

As we read the newspaper, listen to the news reports or just converse with people in general, we hear about all kinds of events and behaviors associated with them. Some of the stories we hear are simply shocking. We may often say, "What in the world were they thinking?" The truth is, in many of those instances, they weren't thinking.

Good or bad, we hear unbelievable stories. There are good stories similar to the "Widows Mite" (someone making an unbelievable sacrifice) and bad stories like a murder suicide (someone taking the lives of innocent family members and then taking their own life) because they decided that was the best way to deal with their life challenge. Either way, the question still comes to mind – "what were they thinking?" We may never know what led them to their decision. We do know, however, that sin is the real cause of destructive behavior and the atoning work of our Lord and Savior Jesus Christ is our solution.

Reverend Gregory L. Williamson

If we go to the Word of God for answers, we can find passages like the scripture referenced above for some solace. The apostle Paul provides a wealth of encouragement, guidance and comfort for life's challenges. He instructs us to Rejoice in the Lord, Live in Moderation, make all of our requests to God by Prayer, Supplication and Thanksgiving and the Peace of God that encompasses our heart and mind will be our result. That advice precedes our theme passage above. He further tells us that this practice will produce contentment, knowing that we can do or endure all things through Christ Jesus because He provides the physical and spiritual strength to find understanding and guidance in all things according to God's will. We know this because God is able and does supply all of our needs according to His riches in Glory.

Yes, all of this instruction is packed in this one chapter of Philippians 4. I am not saying that Paul didn't experience challenges in life. I am not saying that applying these scriptures to your life will assure you of not having challenges in life. What I am saying is that without the help of God through His Holy Spirit, all of us would utterly fall, but His Grace and Mercy are available to us at all times. We may encounter times of discouragement, defeat, helplessness and be tempted to give up and end it all, but we have another option. I Peter 5:7 reminds us to "cast all of our cares upon the Lord because He cares for us. His love, care and concern are never ending.

I don't know what you are thinking right now, but I do have a great suggestion. Whatever your station in life is, remember Paul's advice - whatsoever things are true, whatsoever things are honest, whatsoever things are just, whatsoever things are pure, whatsoever things are lovely, whatsoever things are of good

One Year in Devotional Studies

report, if there be any virtue, and if there be any praise, think on these things. In Jesus Name, Amen.

Daily Devotional Reading

Week 24

- **Monday -** Romans 1:20-32
- **Tuesday -** Philippians 4:8
- **Wednesday -** Job 35:2
- **Thursday -** Proverbs 23:7
- **Friday -** St. Matthew 6:7
- **Saturday -** Zechariah 8:17

One Year in Devotional Studies

Week 25

God's Rivers of Water

⁷ "Blessed is the man that trusteth in the LORD, and whose hope the LORD is. ⁸ For he shall be as a tree planted by the waters, and that spreadeth out her roots by the river, and shall not see when heat cometh, but her leaf shall be green; and shall not be careful in the year of drought, neither shall cease from yielding fruit."

Jeremiah 17:7-8

Whether it's hope and trust or trust and hope, we are all quite familiar with the two. From time to time we have found ourselves in a bind hoping and trusting that things would work out favorably for us. What may separate some of us from others is in what and/or whom we lay our hope and trust. Outside of an epiphany, most of us operate from the base or roots established from our youth. My mode of operation may not make sense to you, and yours may seem strange to me, but our families, culture and upbringing produce the roots from which we work. It may appear strange to some, but it's our norm.

As we grow and mature, those modes of operation are tweaked. That tweaking can make life better, or it can make life more challenging, depending on what it feeds on and how it is interpreted. If we want to consistently grow and mature in a positive and productive manner, we must seek nourishment from

Reverend Gregory L. Williamson

quality sources. Jeremiah encourages us with these words; "Blessed is the man or woman whose trust and hope is in the Lord." He points out a very significant blessing in that this man is much like a tree, planted by rivers of water. That nourishment of water is available all the time enabling them to produce fruit at all times.

I see a huge blessing in this passage. I don't want to be picky, but farmers plant or sow tree seeds. Trees are not planted, they are transplanted. What I like about this is no matter what family you were born into, what kind of living conditions you experienced in your youth; whether a bad job, a bad marriage, a bad past, bad habits, etc., God can and will transplant us in wholesome, God inspired, purpose driven soil and cause our roots to spread into areas never known before, causing us to touch and inspire people we never knew before.

That's true! Don't think just because you have been relying on what seems to be polluted or stagnant water that you have no other options. David confirms these same blessings in Psalms 1. David says this man (or woman) delights in the Lord, meditates in and on His word, and whatever he does will prosper because the Lord knows and plans the way of the righteous. There are a lot of things we can rely on and places we can plant ourselves for nourishment in life, but there is only one place that will truly provide continuous and adequate life sustaining nourishment. That is the rivers of water that only God has and offers freely to us. In Jesus Name, Be Blessed. Amen

One Year in Devotional Studies

Daily Devotional Reading

Week 25

- **Monday -** *Psalms 137:1*
- **Tuesday -** *Joel 3:18*
- **Wednesday -** *St. John 7:38*
- **Thursday -** *Psalms 1:3*
- **Friday -** *Isaiah 41:18*
- **Saturday -** *Psalms 119:136*

 One Year in Devotional Studies

Week 26

WHINING ABOUT OUR DINING

Then the foreign rabble who were traveling with the Israelites began to crave the good things of Egypt, and the people of Israel also began to complain. "Oh, for some meat!" they exclaimed. "We remember all the fish we used to eat for free in Egypt. And we had all the cucumbers, melons, leeks, onions, and garlic that we wanted."

Numbers 11:4-5

As the children of Israel set out on their foreign travel, they certainly complained. The novelty and excitement of being delivered from slavery in Egypt began to wear off once they embarked on their second year of freedom. The wilderness was no easy place to live even when they were settled in camp, but it only took three days on the march before the people began to complain to the Lord about their hardships. Some of the "foreign rabble" in the party became quite outspoken about their preference for Egyptian cuisine, and the Israelites joined in complaining about their steady diet of manna. I suspect many of us who are used to our comfortable lifestyle would have joined in the complaining of the wilderness travelers!

God's plan included redeeming them from Egypt (which he had miraculously accomplished), supporting tens of thousands of people in an inhospitable wilderness, taking them into the Promised Land, and enabling them to overthrow the resident population. For this plan to be accomplished, the Lord required his people's unwavering obedience and unfaltering trust. He was, and is, looking for those who would cooperate rather than complain, who would count their blessings rather than chorus their gripes. While God was focusing on the monumental issues, God's people were whining about dining.

The wisest policy is to get on board with what God is doing, whether or not it makes us comfortable. The best way to get on board with
Him is to trust that He knows what He is doing, to obey what He tells us to do, and to have a thankful attitude for everything He has given us. If we don't, He might become angry with such ungrateful, uncooperative children. He might give us what we want, and then we may discover we don't want it. If we *do* get on board with God, we will arrive in the Promised Land, and that's better than leeks, onions, and garlic. Matthew 6:33 and Psalms 84:11 assures us with these words...

> [33] But seek ye first the kingdom of God, and his righteousness; and all these things shall be added unto you.
>
> For the Lord God is a sun and shield: the Lord will give grace and glory: *no good thing* will he withhold from them that walk uprightly. Psalms 84:11

For the "Believer," God expects us to know and focus on the purpose for which He has planned for us and created within us. This plan is not discovered in an instance nor overnight. It is discovered and realized through an intimate journey of relationship "with Him" and complete trust "in Him." As we submit our will unto His, He will by the Power of the Holy Spirit develop

One Year in Devotional Studies

everything within us that we need to "BE" who He has predestined us "To Be." That is where our focus should be, not on what we are eating, unless it pertains to our "feeding" on the Word of God.

Daily Devotional Reading

Week 26

- **Monday -** *Philippians 2:14*
- **Tuesday -** *Numbers 21:5-6*
- **Wednesday -** *Psalms 142:2*
- **Thursday -** *Acts 25:7*
- **Friday -** *Numbers 11:3*
- **Saturday -** *Matthew 6:11*

One Year in Devotional Studies

Week 27

Character

"A good name is better than Precious Perfume,"
Ecclesiastes 7:1

What is Character and why is it important? Character is made up of mental and moral qualities that make an individual distinctively unique and different from others. This difference does not necessarily mean that one is more right or better than the other, just different. The characteristics of an individual involve things or behavior a person consistently exhibit. So why is character important?

God created mankind to be social and interactive with each other. Man is the only part of God's creation that was designed to continuously grow and develop. Our development depends on our interaction with each other. Character reflects a consistent pattern of development whereby one's qualities can be assessed. While doing this, we are afforded opportunities to share growth by learning from others and assisting others in their growth by lending assistance in nurturing their development. Whether or not we take advantage of these opportunities is a personal decision. When we do, we can develop character. When we don't, we sometimes become a character.

Reverend Gregory L. Williamson

Do you have character or are sometimes being a character? The Message Bible says at Eccl. 7:1a, A good reputation is better than a fat bank account. I think we all can relate to that example. Solomon is encouraging us to develop "character", not to be one. Too many people allow others to define them and tell them who they are. Once we discover who we are in Christ that settles it. That's who we are, even if we don't see the characteristics displayed yet. That just simply means that we have work to do, and don't we all!

When your name is called, what do people think? When you enter the room, what effect does it have on the meeting? When you come to work, are your coworkers happy to see you or do they display a different behavior. None of us had anything to do with the name we have. There are numbers of people that dislike their names for one reason or another. Our name, however, doesn't have to determine our behavior, whether we like our name or not. Determine what God wants from your life, add some other qualities that accent your purpose, and you can honestly tell others, "That's what my name means" because that is what they will see in the life you live. Yes, a good name and reputation are better than precious perfume, or a fat bank account, popularity or any other empty title that the world holds in high esteem. Yes, character is important because Christ is our example and He exhibited character in everything He did. As we reflect the life of Christ in our walk, adding character is both constructive and productive. In Jesus Name, Amen.

One Year in Devotional Studies

Daily Devotional Reading

Week 27

- **Monday -** *Colossians 3:12*
- **Tuesday -** *Philippians 2:19-22*
- **Wednesday -** *Romans 5:4*
- **Thursday -** *2 Samuel 22:31*
- **Friday -** *Acts 17:11*
- **Saturday -** *1 Corinthians 1:26*

One Year in Devotional Studies

Week 28

Discipline Defeats Foolishness

"Foolishness is bound up in the heart of a child, but the ROD of Discipline will drive it far from him."
Proverbs 22:15

Proverbs 22 provides a litany of instructions to rely on to develop quality, substance, character and structure in our lives and for our offspring. The method used is no different than the one God uses with us. Just as our children are to be in submission to us, so are we to live in submission to our heavenly Father. There are five nouns that God uses to parent us, and we can also utilize them to yield successful results with our children. However, our intentions must be like God's. His correction is focused on changing our behavior, not punishment. God uses discipline, dedicated to teach us how to live by the example Christ provided us through the power of love.

Discipline – Choosing and implementing the best corrective method for the individual. There is no one solution that will work for all circumstances. Col. 3:21

Dedication – We must be consistent. If we are not, children become confused and will usually try us. With God, when we instantly don't receive His correction, we think we got away. Prov. 22:6

Teaching – We must use each instance of discipline as an opportunity to teach valuable life principles. Prov. 15:33

Example – One of the most effective vehicles to change is personal accountability. I have learned that some things can't be taught; they must be caught. By caught, I mean contagious. If our children see us practicing what we preach, that carries an enormous amount of weight in our credibility and their commitment to follow that example. I Cor. 11:1

Love – It is true and genuine love (agape) that keeps us in a balanced relationship with God. That same kind of love will keep us in a balanced relationship with our children. If you are not feeling the love, hold off with the discipline or correction until you do. Even if they get away with one, how many did you get away with? I think somewhere along the way, we reap the reward for every deed done, whether good or bad. Eph. 6:4

God wants balance in all of our lives whether we are parents, children, grandchildren or grandparents. He fully knows and understands that we were born with a sin nature and a devilish propensity to display foolishness. However, if we respond to others as He does to us, we can and will drive out the foolishness in our lives with the "rod" or "structure" of discipline. God said it and I believe it. I pray we find all benefit from it. In Jesus Name, Amen.

One Year in Devotional Studies

Daily Devotional Reading

Week 28

- **Monday -** Hebrews 12:11
- **Tuesday -** 1 Corinthians 1:18
- **Wednesday -** Psalms 69:5
- **Thursday -** Job 36:10
- **Friday -** Proverbs 15:14
- **Saturday -** Romans 5:19

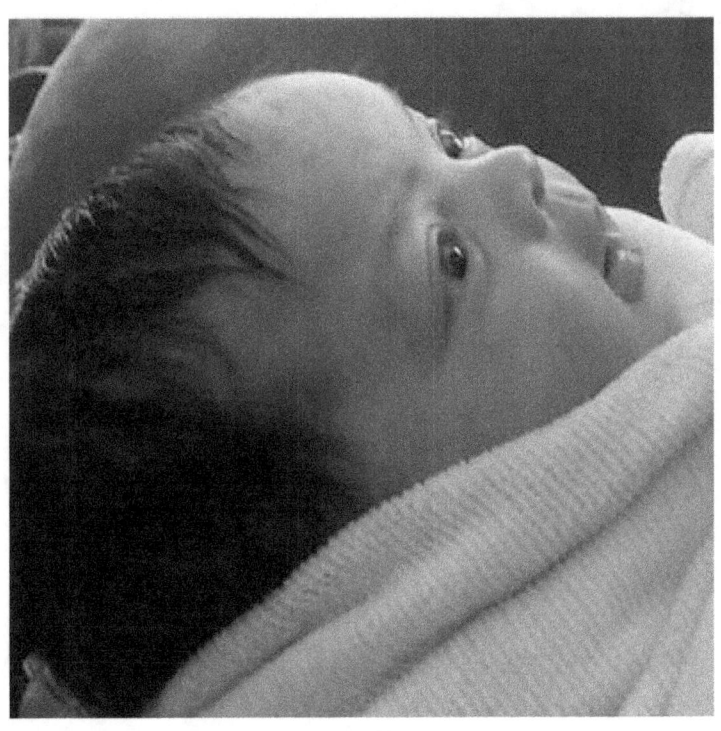

One Year in Devotional Studies

Week 29

Family Inheritance

"He was in the world, and the world was made by him, and the world knew him not. ¹¹ He came unto his own, and his own received him not. ¹² But as many as received him, to them gave He power to become the sons of God, even to them that believe on his name."

St. John 1:10-12

According to Genesis 2:24, Adam and Eve were the first of God's human creation and they were also the first family, established by God. They were not totally perfect but they were totally innocent. They had not been exposed to anything undesirable or displeasing to God. But things would not stay that way.

God gave Adam dominion over all of His creation along with instructions relative to what was good and acceptable and what was prohibited. No matter how you look at it or who you attribute the blame, Eve disobeyed God's command and Adam aborted his responsibility to God's command. After all, God holds each man accountable for the headship of his family. **But I would have you know, that the head of every man is Christ; and the head of the woman is the man; and the head of Christ is God.** (I Cor. 11:3.)

Reverend Gregory L. Williamson

How a man administrates the business of the family is very important because it weighs heavy on how future generations might be affected. It has often been said that when it comes to learning, "more is caught, than taught. Establishing a good practice in the beginning is much more productive and yields greater success than redirecting a bad habit or practice. Solomon reminds us of this at Proverbs 22:6. Cain and Abel's altercation recorded in the fourth chapter of Genesis reveals how fast jealously, envy and discord between family members can evolve and develop into anger, bitterness and violence. This encounter ended in death.

For Disciples of Christ, it should be no secret that Satan's primary target, in his destructive attempts, is the family. In addition, we should know that he focuses on the man or the head of the household. It doesn't take a genius to see that, *"if you weaken the head, the body will soon follow."* Equally important is the fact that a unified family is the strongest group that God established. So true is this statement that even when mankind's intentions were wrong, God still said in Genesis 11:6 - **And the Lord said, Behold, the people is one, and they have all one language; and this they begin to do: and now nothing will be restrained from them, which they have imagined to do.**

If there is one point of focus I can leave with you, it would be this; all of our families have issues. Some may seem worse than others but within each family, these issues, unresolved, can have devastating consequences. When we realize and recognize that in most instances, our family members are not attacking us, they have fallen prey to one of Satan's deceptive schemes. Anger, bitterness and revenge is not going to fix the problem but a unified effort (in fervent prayer) with a common objective (to Glorify God) will squash Satan's plans, Glorify God our Father, and usher us into maturity. When Roman 8:28 says all things work for our good, it's

 One Year in Devotional Studies

this kind of thing that Paul has in mind. *God even orchestrates the devilish attempts of Satan to advance us forward*, if we address them the right way. Further reading from verse 29-37 assures us that we are *adopted members of the family of God with full inheritance*. Because God is for us, no one can effectively stand against us. *We are MORE than conquerors* because He loves us with a never-ending love. We need to show that same kind of love toward our families and especially those of the household of faith. In Jesus Name, Amen.

Daily Devotional Reading

Week 29

- **Monday -** Proverbs 13:22
- **Tuesday -** Exodus 34:9
- **Wednesday -** Galatians 3:18
- **Thursday -** Deuteronomy 18:2
- **Friday -** Acts 20:32
- **Saturday -** 1 Peter 1:3-4

One Year in Devotional Studies

Week 30

Passing the Torch

"Then Moses went and spoke these words to all the Israelites. ² Moses said to them, "I am now 120 years old. I cannot lead you anymore. The LORD said to me, 'You will not go across the Jordan River.' ³ But the LORD your God will lead you people into that land. He will destroy these nations for you. You will take their land away from them. The LORD said that Joshua must lead you.""

Deuteronomy 31:1-3

In this passage, you will find Moses conveying an all important message to Israel that his leadership, as they would know it, had come to its climax. He tells them that Joshua would be the one that would lead them into the Promised Land. Even though Joshua would be the front man, he focuses on the fact that it is Jehovah Himself that will go before them and would have their back. He also assures them more than once that Jehovah would neither leave nor forsake them. They were to be of good courage and not fear.

One thing I gleaned from this passage is the vital importance of learning and observing as much as you can from the various mentors, leaders, pastors, and anybody else that has skills that you don't have. We never know how much time God will allow the many people that pour into our lives to remain in that position. Joshua always showed himself to be someone that Moses could depend on, and most importantly, someone that God could depend on. This was an example of passing the torch.

After the tragic plane crash in 2014 that took the life of Dr. Miles Monroe and others, I listened to a broadcast that Dr. Monroe recorded two weeks prior where he talked about the importance of handing the baton to one's successor with a ceremonial celebration the focus. What seems to happen all too often are leaders dying in the head position (both physically and spiritually) and all of the unnecessary challenges that their successor as well as their followers have to endure.

There may be a torch that's about to be passed in your life. Are you ready and able to receive and run with it? If not, it may be time to make a deeper commitment. May we all deepen our commitment to God. In Jesus Name, Amen.

One Year in Devotional Studies

Daily Devotional Reading

Week 30

- **Monday -** Genesis 48:6
- **Tuesday -** Numbers 18:20
- **Wednesday -** Joshua 14:9
- **Thursday -** St. Matthew 28:18-20
- **Friday -** Joshua 1:2-5
- **Saturday -** Genesis 49:33

One Year in Devotional Studies

Week 31

The Person Behind the Name

"And when eight days were accomplished for the circumcising of the child, His name was called Jesus, which was so named of the angel before he was conceived in the womb."

St. Luke 2:21

Throughout history there have been common names that are unique to a certain generation or period of time. Choose a period of time and you will find a common theme or thread associated with the names people ascribed to their children. History reveals that during the most recent slave era, Sir Names were associated with slave owners. First names, most often had something to do with a person's physical characteristics. The Native American Indian names were much like this. The list of reasons, perspectives and factors that determine or aid in determining how names are chosen is endless. All of that being said, none of these methods are as effective as the one the Bible utilizes.

The Bible illustrates that the most effective method was to first, thank God for the gift of new life and also entrusting them with the responsibility of guiding that life. Secondly, by dedicating that life to God with the focus placed on raising the child with a mindset to glorify God. After all, that is our main purpose in and for life. Those

Reverend Gregory L. Williamson

in scripture that followed this practice consulted God for the proper name to give to their children.

When Zacharias and Elisabeth were blessed with the awesome gift of "John the Baptizer", they didn't do as so many of us do; "since it's a boy, we will name him Zack Jr. after his father." At Luke 1:13 we find these words; But the angel said unto him, Fear not, Zacharias: for thy prayer is heard; and thy wife Elisabeth shall bear thee a son, and thou shalt call his name John. God had directed them, *through the aiding of the Holy Spirit*, what name they should give their child before he was even born. With a relationship with God and an ear to hear, they were obedient to the guiding of the Holy Spirit. The end result of John's life was tragic but the blessing from their obedience was unmatched. Luke 7:28a says, For I say unto you, Among those that are born of women there is not a greater prophet than John the Baptist.

The topic for this devotional is "the person behind the name." I questioned however whether or not that should have been "the name behind the person." I chose this topic because in our society, we attribute greatness to a person's name after they obtain what we call success. They then become the person behind that great name. The Bible rather chooses a great name and a great purposeful meaning in that name and then attach it to a person, thereby indicating the desire and expectation of greatness from that individual. That, I believe, is a much better approach.

Robert Rosenthal and Lenore Jackson said, Parent's expectations and reinforcement of their kids (especially before age eight) strongly influence their character and behavior. I fully understand that some people succeed in spite of their opposition and our names are just one factor in reflecting greatness. However, if we desire greatness from them, why not give them a name, *from their very beginning*, that depicts the purposeful greatness that God has

One Year in Devotional Studies

planned for their life. Even if we have children with names that may not convey a message of greatness, we can redefine the meaning of their name and speak greatness unto their lives. Then, the person behind the name and the name behind the person will both reflect greatness. Prayerfully, it will also Glorify Our Heavenly Father. In Jesus Name, Amen.

Daily Devotional Reading

Week 31

- **Monday -** Proverbs 22:1
- **Tuesday -** Genesis 3:20
- **Wednesday -** St. James 5:14
- **Thursday -** Exodus 3:13
- **Friday -** Genesis 17:5
- **Saturday -** Philippians 2:9-10

One Year in Devotional Studies

Week 32

We Are Family

"Something from the Spirit can be seen in each person. The Spirit gives this to each one to help others. ⁸ The Spirit gives one person the ability to speak with wisdom. And the same Spirit gives another person the ability to speak with knowledge. ⁹ The same Spirit gives faith to one person and to another he gives gifts of healing. ¹⁰ The Spirit gives to one person the power to do miracles, to another the ability to prophesy, and to another the ability to judge what is from the Spirit and what is not. The Spirit gives one person the ability to speak in different kinds of languages, and to another the ability to interpret those languages. ¹¹ One Spirit, the same Spirit, does all these things. The Spirit decides what to give each one."

I Corinthians 12:8-11

The verses above are lengthy, but I needed to make sure the entire message Paul intended to send was effectively conveyed. It should be no secret that God, our Maker and Creator is all about family. Not only does He want to have a family relationship with us, He also wants us to utilize the idea and concept of family. Naturally, He wants that arrangement in our personal families. Even as it relates to our churches, our schools, our neighborhoods, work environment, etc., He wants the believer to operate from a family perspective.

From the beginning of creation, we see God's arrangement for family with Adam and Eve. It continued with Able, Cain, and Seth. Noah and his family and God's involvement with them are well documented in scripture. The list continues in so many ways, large families (12 sons of Jacob) to small families (Samson and John the Baptist), single parents (Timothy), grandmothers and Blended families (the 12 disciples). The disciples is the family I want to focus on.

When Jesus chose these twelve men, we discover in the end that one of them betrayed Jesus; it was Judas, yet Jesus still chose him. We see a variety of personalities and behaviors in these twelve men, but they were the twelve Jesus chose. Some were better than others at some things, some were closer to Jesus than others, but they were all His chosen disciples.

The verses above from I Corinthians 12 reveal the importance of the diversity among the disciples. They convey to us that first of all, God gives or establishes gifts in each one of us by means of the same Holy Spirit. Secondly, He distributes those gifts based on His purpose for our life. Thirdly, He calls us to a purpose that is larger than we are to show us that we need each other as well as each other's gifting. God provides everything within the person to fulfill everything He calls you to do or to be.

Jesus called 12 ordinary men, and through them, accomplished extraordinary results. Even the lessons we learn from Judas are invaluable. Let's focus so strongly on what gifts God has given us that we find no time to envy others' gifting. Then we can work together as one family in Christ as God intended. In Jesus Name, Amen.

One Year in Devotional Studies

Daily Devotional Reading

Week 32

- **Monday -** *Proverbs 22:1*
- **Tuesday -** *Genesis 3:20*
- **Wednesday -** *St. James 5:14*
- **Thursday -** *Exodus 3:13*
- **Friday -** *Genesis 17:5*
- **Saturday -** *Philippians 2:9-10*

One Year in Devotional Studies

Week 33

Illuminating a Dark Day

⁵⁴ "Upon hearing this, his audience could contain themselves no longer. They boiled in fury at Stephen; they clenched their jaws and ground their teeth. ⁵⁵ But Stephen was filled with the Holy Spirit. Gazing upward into heaven, he saw something they couldn't see: the glory of God, and Jesus standing at His right hand. The whole crowd rushed at Stephen, converged on him, ⁵⁸ dragged him out of the city, and stoned him ⁵⁹ while they were pelting Stephen with rocks. Stephen replied: Lord Jesus, receive my spirit. ⁶⁰ Then he knelt in prayer, shouting at the top of his lungs, Lord, do not hold this evil against them! After these final words, Stephen fell asleep in death."

Acts 7:54-60

On September 11, 2001, 19 militants associated with the Islamic extremist group al-Qaeda hijacked four airliners and carried out suicide attacks against targets in the United States. Over 3,000 people were killed during the attacks in New York City and Washington, D.C., including more than 400 police officers and firefighters. September 11, 2001, was the deadliest day in history for New York City firefighters: 343 were killed.

Operation Enduring Freedom, the American-led international effort to oust the Taliban regime in Afghanistan and destroy Osama bin Laden's terrorist network based there, began on October 7. Within two months, U.S. forces had effectively removed the

Taliban from operational power, but the war continued, as U.S. and coalition forces attempted to defeat a Taliban insurgency campaign based in neighboring Pakistan. Osama bin Laden, the mastermind behind the September 11th attacks, remained at large until May 2, 2011, when he was finally tracked down and killed by U.S. forces at a hideout in Abbottabad, Pakistan. In June 2011, President Barack Obama announced the beginning of large-scale troop withdrawals from Afghanistan, with a final withdrawal of U.S. forces tentatively scheduled for 2014.

On this September 11, 2015 morning, victims' families will gather for a reading of the names of the nearly 3,000 people killed in the terror strike. Observances are planned around the country, including the two other places where hijacked planes crashed on Sept. 11, 2001 — at the Pentagon and near Shanksville, Pennsylvania. For many of these families, if not all, this day will be remembered as one of the darkest days in our history but putting all things in perspective, "Respectfully", is it really?

Our focus scripture depicts the martyred death of Stephen. More importantly however is the example of our Lord and Savior, Jesus Christ, who was crucified because of His love and compassion for mankind. Although He was not guilty of any wrong, He personally paid the ultimate price for the sins of the world, in spite of the hated exhibited toward Him. He provoke the same kind of anger, hatred, bigotry and bitterness that led to Stephen's stoning. However, neither He nor Stephen allowed this evil behavior to destroy their love, devotion and commitment to their Sovereign King, Jehovah Elohim. "Even when we don't understand why, God still has a purpose!"

As we remember September 11, 2001 and the lives of the 3000 that were unnecessarily cut short, let's keep their families and friends as well as our entire Nation lifted up in prayer. This was just one horrific example of what anger, bitterness and confusion

One Year in Devotional Studies

can lead to. Yes it was a "Dark Day" in our history but so was the day we call "Good Friday." Good Friday however, led to the illumination of "Resurrection Sunday." [9] May we never tire of doing what is good and right before our Lord because in His season we shall bring in a great harvest if we can just persist (Gal. 6:9). In Jesus Name, Amen.

Daily Devotional Reading

Week 33

- **Monday -** St. John 8:12
- **Tuesday -** Genesis 1:3
- **Wednesday -** Exodus 13:21
- **Thursday -** Job 30:26
- **Friday -** Psalms 27:1
- **Saturday -** Ephesians 5:8

One Year in Devotional Studies

Week 34

Defining Storms

"Then they cry unto the LORD in their trouble, and he bringeth them out of their distresses. ²⁹ He maketh the storm a calm, so that the waves thereof are still. ³⁰ Then are they glad because they be quiet; so he bringeth them unto their desired haven."

Psalms 107:28-30

Webster defines a storm as - a disturbance of the atmosphere marked by wind and usually by rain, snow, hail, sleet, or thunder and lightning. Probably all of us have seen storms that would fit this description. Many of us have seen storms that were rare, unique, strange or perplexing. Maybe a snow storm where the temperature was above 32 degrees. A hail storm that came from out of nowhere in the spring of the year. How we define a storm has a lot to do with the experiences we've had, relative to storms.

In the gospel of Mark, the disciples had an encounter with a storm. In fact, the Word of God says at Mark 4:37 that it was a great storm, so much so that the waves beat into the boat. This had to be a terrible storm because the scripture goes on to say that they became afraid. Ordinarily, that might not carry so much weight but because many of the disciples were fishermen, they had, I'm sure, encountered storms of some type before. However, maybe never a storm like this one. This was a storm of a different kind.

Some of us have experienced different kinds of storms as well. Storms unlike any that we've seen before. Storms that seem to be life threatening. How would you define those kinds of storms? The Word of God defines them as defining moments of character creation, integrity establishing and most importantly, relationship builders.

These storms occur on the inside, not in the atmosphere. They dig deep into our innermost parts and sometimes cause us to question whether or not God really loves us. Does He really care about me? Is He really aware of what I am going through? Does He really have the power to put a stop to this when I've reached my breaking point? Does He know that I'm at my breaking point? What is my breaking point? The list of questions could go on forever so let me address them.

I was told years ago, "Storms in Life Will Strengthen you, If They Don't Crush You." What the heck does that mean? When we keep our focus on what we know by experience and what we know through the word of God, Storms will strengthen us. We must remember that we are not exempt from storms (John 16:33). Sometimes we create our own storms (Jeremiah 16:11-13). Albeit, no storm is too big for our God (Luke 1:37). We grow closer in our love, trust and understanding of God through storms (Matt. 8:27). The celebration intensifies after coming out of a storm (I Peter 1:6-7). James 1:2 says Count it all joy and we can, when we properly define the storm and its purpose. In Jesus Name, Amen.

One Year in Devotional Studies

Daily Devotional Reading

Week 34

- **Monday -** *Isaiah 25:4*
- **Tuesday -** *Ezekiel 13:11-13*
- **Wednesday -** *St. Matthew 8:23-27*
- **Thursday -** *Nahum 1:3*
- **Friday -** *Psalms 107:29*
- **Saturday -** *St. Matthew 16:3*

One Year in Devotional Studies

Week 35

What Are You Standing On?

"And being fully persuaded that, what he had promised, he was able also to perform."

Romans 4:21

From a builder's perspective, a foundation is the lowest load bearing part of a building, typically below ground level. In a basic sense, it would be like a footing or the concrete beneath a basement or slab that provides a stable base for the house. Another definition is, an underlying basis or principle for something. This definition speaks to the principle reasoning behind a decision made or a position taken. The latter is more in line with the direction of thought to which the Apostle Paul is speaking.

All of us at some point find ourselves in need of assistance with something that we can't fix, handle, or resolve on our own. If we seek assistance from another source, we will usually encounter one of four variables: someone willing to help but doesn't have the resources, someone that has the resources but is unwilling to help, someone that has neither resources nor willingness, or the last option and best scenario, someone that has both the resources and the willingness to provide the necessary assistance. How do you know which one you have?

Reverend Gregory L. Williamson

There is really only one person you can go to that will always have both the resources and the desire to help. Equally important, this person will always have the ability to not only resolve our problems but also bring about the best result for us (Romans 8:28). This person is our Heavenly Father, Almighty God, The Omniscient One. God knows our needs before we even realize that we have any. As we trust and rely on Him as our Jehovah Jireh (Our Provider), our faith and confidence in Him should consistently increase because He will never fail us or let us down.

He may not transcendentally appear and zap your problems away, but He will send someone that He has motivated, equipped, instructed and prepared to administer just what is needed to eradicate your situation. Moreover, He compassionately provides sufficient grace to cope with the problem until He dissolves it. That's why we read the words Paul inscribed above about Abraham in verse 21.

Abraham had no reservations about believing God and His promises. All of the promises God made to Abraham, He fulfilled. The Bible says "it" or "his faith" was imputed or accounted to him for righteousness. Because we are heirs of Abraham, those same promises and more are promised to us. We can stand on those same principles, promises and declarations of God. And when we do, we will be successful in our endeavors because God's word never fails. May we continue to find comfort and great foundational footing in the word of God. In Jesus name, Amen.

One Year in Devotional Studies

Daily Devotional Reading

Week 35

- **Monday -** 2 Chronicles 8:16
- **Tuesday -** Ezra 3:10
- **Wednesday -** Job 38:4
- **Thursday -** St. Matthew 13:35
- **Friday -** Psalms 11:3
- **Saturday -** 1 Timothy 6:19

Reverend Gregory L. Williamson

One Year in Devotional Studies

Week 36

The Presence of "The LORD"

The angels were calling to each other, "Holy, holy, holy is the LORD All-Powerful. His Glory fills the whole earth."

Isaiah 6:3

Every experience where someone had an encounter with "The presence of God," it was for a specific God-designed purpose. I have on occasion heard people make reference to a time when they or someone else was in the presence of the lord. I'm sure all of them has to be an awesome experience. Why? Because the "Presence of God" experiences mentioned in scripture are just earth shaking. Think about when God called to Adam and asked – "Where are you Adam?" The time Moses was intrigued by the burning bush only to find himself in the very "Presence of God." Paul's experience on the Damascus road. The experiences of Elijah, Daniel, the three Hebrew boys, Peter, James and John on the mountain of transfiguration, John in Revelation, and the list could go on and on, hopefully including you and I somewhere along the way.

Yes, the presence of the Lord is a very powerful and humbling experience. It might bring about fear, tears, or trembling, but ultimately, it produces a sense of honor, reverence and respect at an awesome level, unmatched by anything we have ever known. Whether you have experienced this or not, one thing is for sure, there is no reason for alarm. We know from God's word that he is ever present with us at all times.

We probably couldn't take it if we had the kind of experiences described in scripture every minute of our lives. Our bodies would probably explode. Nevertheless, I desire it as often as God is willing to let me in because in all truth and reality, *there is no better place to be.* I encourage you to read and meditate on the passages below and see if you find yourself in the very presence of God.

- There shall not any man be able to stand before thee all the days of thy life: as I was with Moses, so I will be with thee: I will not fail thee, nor forsake thee. Joshua 1:5 and 9

- Have not I commanded thee? Be strong and of a good courage; be not afraid, neither be thou dismayed: for the Lord thy God is with thee whithersoever thou goest.

- When mine enemies are turned back, they shall fall and perish at thy presence. Psa 9:3

- Thou wilt shew me the path of life: in thy presence is fulness of joy; at thy right hand there are pleasures for evermore. Psa 16:11

- Thou preparest a table before me in the presence of mine enemies: thou anointest my head with oil; my cup runneth over. Psa. 23:5

- Now unto him that is able to keep you from falling, and to present you faultless before the presence of his glory with exceeding joy - Jude 1:24

One Year in Devotional Studies

Daily Devotional Reading

Week 36

- **Monday -** *Psalms 16*
- **Tuesday -** *Genesis 3:8*
- **Wednesday -** *1 Chronicles 16:27*
- **Thursday -** *Job 1:12*
- **Friday -** *Psalms 68:2*
- **Saturday -** *Acts 3:19*

One Year in Devotional Studies

Week 37

Wisdom's Response

"Even a fool, when he holdeth his peace, is counted wise: and he that shutteth his lips is esteemed a man of understanding."

Proverbs 17:28

Many of us grew up learning either by being taught to speak up or by perceiving that those who spoke up usually came out on top. In addition to that, it seemed that if both parties spoke up, then those that spoke the loudest came out on top. Thus, today we see the fruits of that teaching: people yelling at each other at the top of their lungs to overshadow the words of their opponent.

I know this reminds you of grade school experiences. Unfortunately, this is very common in adult life as well "now." In the book of Ecclesiastes, Solomon speaks to varying benefits of wisdom and how it can and will guide you successfully through life, if properly utilized. In chapter 3, verse 7, he focuses on timing. When wisdom and timing are properly connected, the result is usually a very powerful one.

Many people have been left looking silly and dumbfounded as a result of someone cleverly and astutely utilizing wisdom and timing. I remember many years ago listening to a middle school

Reverend Gregory L. Williamson

principal mitigating after two girls (classmates) had been fighting and were brought to the office for discipline. In his investigative questioning, he asked "What caused the fight to start?" The answer was, "She called me out of my name." He asked the same question three time and got the same answer, "She called me out of my name." He finally asked, what did she call you? She replied "an expletive." He then asked, are you a "that expletive"? She said NO! He then told her there was no need for her to fight. She said she was taught to always stand up for herself. The principal said there is nothing wrong with standing up for yourself, but I asked you if you were an expletive and you said NO! So my question to you is, "Why did you respond?" She was obviously talking to someone else. I thought that was good wisdom.

I have learned in life that every question directed at me doesn't warrant an answer from me. When we learn to apply God's word (which is His wisdom) to life's encounters, we too will discern the times when we should offer a wise response and times when we are best to ignore the ignorance of what is said and move on. The wise words stated in the referenced scripture above is very true. Many unlearned men and women have been thought wise because of their silence. Maybe that's where the saying "Silence is Golden" came from. We should always choose our battles wisely. Allowing others to demand a response from us at every question gives them control over our lives. Only God deserves that position in our lives. Be Blessed and Be Encouraged in Jesus Name, Amen.

One Year in Devotional Studies

Daily Devotional Reading

Week 37

- **Monday -** *St. James 1:5*
- **Tuesday -** *Exodus 28:13*
- **Wednesday -** *1 Kings 3:28*
- **Thursday -** *Colossians 3:16*
- **Friday -** *2 Corinthians 1:12*
- **Saturday -** *St. Matthew 13:54*

One Year in Devotional Studies

Week 38

A Work Around

³⁷ "Now when they heard this, they were pricked in their heart, and said unto Peter and to the rest of the apostles, Men and brethren, what shall we do? ⁴⁴ And all that believed were together, and had all things common; ⁴⁵ And sold their possessions and goods, and parted them to all men, as every man had need."

Acts 2:37 and 44-45

We have a term at work we refer to as a "work around." A work around comes into play when something (computer program, an engineered part, individual, etc.) doesn't function as it was expected, intended or designed to. Other means of accomplishing the desired outcome is implemented. This doesn't usually obtain the same outcome but it's usually a workable substitute.

"Work Arounds" most often come about when a failure occurs in a previously designed process. In the book of Acts, we can find a similar situation in Acts 2. Peter describes an opportunity that Jesus provided and continues to provide that depicts the lifestyle or life course of a believer. After choosing a different course of action or a "Work Around", many of the vary Jewish believers that once followed Jesus and His teachings, veered off course and became guilty of supporting the crucifixion of Jesus Christ. They didn't openly say, Crucify Him" but they did not speak out against it either. Failing to speak out against injustice can and often will lead to supporting the very injustice that we preach and teach against. As devastating as this can be, we are all capable of doing the same thing, we're human! When we find ourselves in those kinds of situations, we must recognize our wrong and begin the necessary steps to correct it. We have heard many clichés that fit into this category; if you don't stand for something, you will fall for anything. If you are not part of the solution, you are part of the problem. Even when we are silent, we still send a message. That being said, there is a process to correction and it must be followed completely if we intend to get the complete results. However, many times impatience causes us to skip steps and/or add unnecessary steps that becomes our "Work Around". The end result is the frustration that comes from a partial fix.

After Peter explained to these believers that they were guilty of crucifying Christ, many of them (not all of them) were pricked in their hearts (convicted). Their response was, Brothers, what shall we do? Peter said that they must "Repent, Be Baptized in Jesus Name for Forgiveness of their sin and then receive the Holy Spirit for Power, Guidance and Direction. Not everyone received his message but those that did, they continually committed themselves to learning what the apostles taught them, gathering for fellowship, breaking bread, and praying. There was an intense sense of togetherness among all who believed; they shared all their material possessions in trust. They were unified. They shared meals together. With gladness, they worshiped God with generous hearts. The new disciples praised God, and the Lord added to their number everyone who was experiencing freedom and liberation. I pray we may also see the unspeakable and incomparable value of staying with God's plan and not choosing a "Work Around"? In Jesus Name, Amen.

One Year in Devotional Studies

Daily Devotional Reading

Week 38

- **Monday -** Genesis 18:15
- **Tuesday -** St. John 12:27-28
- **Wednesday -** Acts 5:3
- **Thursday -** Genesis 4:6-7
- **Friday -** Numbers 14:33
- **Saturday -** Acts 1:26

One Year in Devotional Studies

Week 39

What's Most Important?

"The one who plants and the one who waters work as a team with the same purpose . . . We work together as partners who belong to God. You are God's field, God's building—not ours. Because of God's special favor to me, I have laid the foundation like an expert builder."

1 Corinthians 3:8-10

Any building erected without an adequate foundation cannot stand. Equally true is, any church that gets away from loving, worshiping, and serving the Lord Jesus cannot honestly claim to be a genuine church. We must always remember that it's the people that make the church, not just the brick and mortar. How we function within the church determines the foundation and perception of the church. Everyone's work will be put through the fire to see whether or not it keeps its value (I Cor. 3:13). Jesus's words at Matthew 7:24-27 reminds us of how devastating the results of poor planning can be.

Church life is neither mundane nor routine - it is God's work. We're building God's building, and he expects quality workmanship. Great care has to be exercised to ensure that a proper foundation is laid and built upon. The only legitimate foundation for the church is "Jesus Christ" (I Cor. 3:11).

We also see at I Cor. 12:12 -

> *"For as the body is one, and hath many members, and all the members of that one body, being many, are one body: so also is Christ."*

In conclusion, let me point out that the church is comprised of the people, not the building. Sanctified people sanctify the building. Because the church is the Body of Christ, He provides everything necessary for the success of the church. He does this by infusing various gifts, talents and abilities to its members. Much like our physical bodies, we are not all hands, feet, eyes, ears, etc., but a combination of all necessary parts to make a whole properly functioning person or "body." No one part can function on its own and no one part or member is more important than another. Our parts are at their best when they are operating in their proper place.

We must stay connected to God. Jesus reminds us at John 15:5, that we can do nothing unless we are connected to Him. He is the one that causes growth. Paul reminds us that we are to plant and water seeds. Growth will occur when God purposes it. The main point is although no one is more important that the other, we are all very important in the work of God. May we be committed to the call that God has placed on our lives and realize that collectively working in unity with other believers will have the greater impact on the Body of Christ. That is the real foundation. Be Blessed in the Lord. In Jesus name, Amen.

One Year in Devotional Studies

Daily Devotional Reading

Week 39

- **Monday -** *St. Matthew 6:33*
- **Tuesday -** *Joshua 24:15*
- **Wednesday -** *St. Luke 9:23*
- **Thursday -** *Colossians 3:1*
- **Friday -** *St. John 12:3*
- **Saturday -** *Revelation 2:4*

One Year in Devotional Studies

Week 40

My "Real" Objective

"And all the congregation said, Amen, and praised the LORD. And the people did according to this promise."

Nehemiah 5:13

Followers of Jesus Christ understand that "amen" in its basic definition means – yes, I agree, so be it, etc. Maybe more academically stated, it denotes a positive affirmation of agreement. If you have ever witnessed the damage and devastation that often occur when Christian brothers and sisters attack each other, then I'm sure you would agree that it's well past the need for Christian brothers and sisters to put an end to the negative attacks we bring on each other. Regardless of our situations and positions in life, none of us is any better than the other.

Given the right challenge, all of us are just one situation away from falling apart. All of us have more than likely witnessed some great, dynamic, Hercules-like individual that was seen in most minds as an unconquerable icon. Some of them were entertainers, business moguls, Pastors of Mega churches, great military leaders, and the list goes on. Yet, like Samson, the most unsuspecting challenge brought them down.

Reverend Gregory L. Williamson

In the passage above we find Nehemiah troubled by the actions of Jewish brethren in terms of how they were treating their fellow Jews, much like the troubling pernicious actions that take place in our political environment during political campaigns. I don't want to get off track; therefore will just make this point: regardless of party affiliation, the focus should be geared toward providing opportunity for all people to improve their condition in life, not using people to better our own station in life. Nehemiah recognized that there were Jews that were in dire straits, mainly financial issues. He did not object to the borrowers being charged interest on what they borrowed. What he did take issue with is the level of interest they assessed.

They pretended that they were concerned about their brothers and wanted to help so they loaned them the resources to get it together. But, was that their "REAL" objective? NO! The real objective was to use these people's hardship to produce personal wealth at their expense. The level of interest these Jews assessed, Nehemiah called "Usury," and it connotes the meaning that it sounds like: using. Even today when people fall into financial troubles, creditors call and/or send all sorts of inducements disguised as help but can act as anchors that are sometimes permanently attached to their necks. Are they really wanting to help? Not really. They are using them and anyone else that buy in, to get rich off of their misfortune.

When we do what we do for those whom we do it for, "What Is our Real Objective?" I pray it is to help improve the conditions of those in need. In Jesus Name, Amen.

One Year in Devotional Studies

Daily Devotional Reading

Week 40

- **Monday -** *Proverbs 16:2*
- **Tuesday -** *Isaiah 1:18*
- **Wednesday -** *1 Samuel 12:7*
- **Thursday -** *Job 32:11*
- **Friday -** *St. Luke 5:21*
- **Saturday -** *1 Peter 3:15*

One Year in Devotional Studies

Week 41

Fear Not, It Is Written!

"Then saith Jesus unto him, Get thee hence, Satan: for it is written, Thou shalt worship the Lord thy God, and him only shalt thou serve. Then the devil leaveth him, and, behold, angels came and ministered unto him."

St. Matthew 4:10-11

Fear is something that all believers deal with at one time or another. I know there are some that will tell you, Not Me, God said it and I believe it. That is very true and a great attitude to have. However, if we would never experience fear, there would not have been any reason for God's word to address it in so many passages, like in the book of Joshua and others. May we all find comfort in God's word when we encounter fear. That's why "It Is Written."

Genesis 15:1
After these things the word of the LORD came unto Abram in a vision, saying, "Fear not, Abram: I am thy shield, and thy exceeding great reward."

Joshua 8:1
And the LORD said unto Joshua, "Fear not, neither be thou

dismayed: take all the people of war with thee, and arise, go up to Ai: see, I have given into thy hand the king of Ai, and his people, and his city, and his land."

Ruth 3:11
"And now, my daughter, fear not; I will do to thee all that thou requirest: for all the city of my people doth know that thou art a virtuous woman."

Isaiah 41:10
"Fear thou not; for I am with thee: be not dismayed; for I am thy God: I will strengthen thee; yea, I will help thee; yea, I will uphold thee with the right hand of my righteousness."

2 Kings 6:16
"And he answered, Fear not: for they that be with us are more than they that be with them."

St. Luke 12:32
"Fear not, little flock; for it is your Father's good pleasure to give you the kingdom."

Revelation 1:17
"And when I saw him, I fell at his feet as dead. And he laid his right hand upon me, saying unto me, Fear not; I am the first and the last:"

These are just a few passages of scripture from Genesis to Revelation that provide believers with encouragement and reassurance when fear shows up in our lives. I pray that you find comfort in these words. In Jesus Name, Amen.

 One Year in Devotional Studies

Daily Devotional Reading
Week 41

- **Monday -** St. Matthew 4:10
- **Tuesday -** Isaiah 41:40
- **Wednesday -** Exodus 24:12
- **Thursday -** 2 Chronicles 20:17
- **Friday -** St. Luke 4:4
- **Saturday -** Psalms 27:3

One Year in Devotional Studies

Week 42

Only By Faith!

"For ye have need of patience, that, after ye have done the will of God, ye might receive the promise."
Hebrews 10:36

The writer of Hebrews is telling us that when we consider all that God has done for us in the past, it would be senseless to throw it all away and lose our promised reward. We just need to utilize patience. This kind of patience comes only by faith.

In all actuality, there are only three ways one can respond to the promises of God: (1) Wait for the promise to occur and give God praise for it. (2) Wait for the promise to occur and never acknowledge that it was God's doing. (3) lastly, and most importantly, Praise God in advance for the Promise and wait for its manifestation. Of course, the last one is the one that God cherishes the most.

Be those believers that trust Him so much that they praise Him for what He has promised, knowing that God will not withhold any good thing from them. I recently attended a revival service where the message was taken from I Kings 17:10-16. *You really need to read those verses.*

[10] "So he arose and went to Zarephath. And when he came to the gate of the city, behold, the widow woman was there gathering of sticks: and he called to her, and said, Fetch me, I pray thee, a little water in a vessel, that I may drink. [11] And as she was going to fetch it, he called to her, and said, Bring me, I pray thee, a morsel of bread in thine hand. [12] And she said, As the LORD thy God liveth, I have not a cake, but an handful of meal in a barrel, and a little oil in a cruse: and, behold, I am gathering two sticks, that I may go in and dress it for me and my son, that we may eat it, and die. [13] And Elijah said unto her, Fear not; go and do as thou hast said: but make me thereof a little cake first, and bring it unto me, and after make for thee and for thy son. [14] For thus saith the LORD God of Israel, The barrel of meal shall not waste, neither shall the cruse of oil fail, until the day that the LORD sendeth rain upon the earth. [15] And she went and did according to the saying of Elijah: and she, and he, and her house, did eat many days. [16] And the barrel of meal wasted not, neither did the cruse of oil fail, according to the word of the LORD, which he spake by Elijah."

If you read those verses, you should understand that the major point made was that by Faith, this widow woman obeyed the word of God through the prophet Elijah at a point when she appeared to be her end. Yet, because of her FAITH and OBEIDIENCE, look what God did. He didn't give her abundance. He sustained what she already had so that it never ran out. Does God need to place a huge amount of money in your bank account, or does He just need to have the money in the account to cover every check you write? Interesting concept isn't it? It Only Happens By Faith. In Jesus Name, Amen.

One Year in Devotional Studies

Daily Devotional Reading

Week 42

- **Monday -** *Romans 10:17*
- **Tuesday -** *St. Mark 10:52*
- **Wednesday -** *St. Matthew 8:10*
- **Thursday -** *Ephesians 2:8*
- **Friday -** *Acts 6:8*
- **Saturday -** *2 Timothy 2:22*

One Year in Devotional Studies

Week 43

God Changes Things

"He wanted to see who Jesus was. There were many others who wanted to see Jesus too. Zacchaeus was too short to see above the people."

St. Luke 19:3

Jesus was going through the city of Jericho. ² In Jericho there was a man named Zacchaeus. He was a wealthy, very important tax collector. ³ He wanted to see who Jesus was. There were many others who wanted to see Jesus too. Zacchaeus was too short to see above the people. ⁴ So he ran to a place where he knew Jesus would come. Then he climbed a sycamore tree so he could see him. ⁵ When Jesus came to where Zacchaeus was, he looked up and saw him in the tree. Jesus said, "Zacchaeus, hurry! Come down! I must stay at your house today." ⁶ Zacchaeus hurried and came down. He was happy to have Jesus in his house. ⁷ Everyone saw this. They began to complain, "Look at the kind of man Jesus is staying with. Zacchaeus is a sinner!" Luke 19:1-7

Varying views and perspectives in life cause many of us to categorize "prominent" people differently. In spite of our differences, all of us will make some exceptions to see, touch or get near a person we deem "prominent." In the passage of scripture above, Jesus is viewed as a "Prominent" person. The crowd of people with Him and those in the path expecting Him reveal that. This passage focuses on one individual that was in that crowd, Zacchaeus. Zacchaeus was also a man of prominence, but Jesus chose to have a personal interaction with him on that day.

The scripture tells us that Zacchaeus was a man short in stature and could not see Jesus because of the crowd. The scripture does not tell us why Zacchaeus pursued Jesus so aggressively. Usually when people made great efforts to get to Jesus, it was because of a need, such as health, financial, protection from a broken law, etc. Since the passage doesn't list a reason, I won't assume one. What I will do, however, is refer to another passage to rationally make a point.

At John 9:1-3, we find this event – "And as Jesus passed by, he saw a man which was blind from his birth. And his disciples asked him, saying, Master, who did sin, this man, or his parents, that he was born blind? Jesus answered, Neither hath this man sinned, nor his parents: *but that the works of God should be made manifest in him."*

Zacchaeus was a Tax Collector. He was wealthy. He was a sinner. Those three things the scripture tells us. Tax collectors were despised in that day. Most of the wealthy oppressed the people so they weren't seen in the greatest light either. Lastly, he was a sinner, and the teachings of the Pharisees all but despised interaction with sinners. Here we have Jesus choosing to go home with someone that possessed all three of these "negative" qualities. What is going on here? God chooses to move on issues quite often to manifest the greatness of God and remind us that nothing is impossible with God. May we rest in knowing that our God is always there when we need Him. Be Blessed In Jesus Name, Amen.

One Year in Devotional Studies

Daily Devotional Reading

Week 43

- **Monday -** *St. Mark 4:39*
- **Tuesday -** *Exodus 10:19*
- **Wednesday -** *Job 14:14*
- **Thursday -** *Ecclesiastes 8:1*
- **Friday -** *Romans 1:26*
- **Saturday -** *Daniel 5:6*

One Year in Devotional Studies

Week 44

Preparation for Running

"Let us lay aside every weight, and the sin which doth so easily beset us, and let us run with patience the race that is set before us,"
Hebrews 12:1

This passage in Hebrews uses the analogy of the precautions a runner takes and the adjustments a runner makes in preparation for a race. In addition to the dietary adjustments of proper eating to provide that extra boost and the physical training to build strength and stamina, the runner also analyzes his equipment to make sure he's getting the best support and the least amount of added weight in exchange for it. Sometimes the difference in who wins and who loses in competitive racing is determined by hundredths of a second. Every ounce counts and has to be calculated. The weight you take into the race has to be carried during the race.

The writer of Hebrews focusses on the spiritual race that the believer runs. This race, in some respects, is an uphill run. It is not run without resistance. Although Satan is very much behind it, he uses urges, desires, fatigue, and every kind of sinful enticement he thinks will slow you down, to get you off course, and ultimately cause you to quit. What he may have failed to realize is that not only are we not running this race alone, there are some in attendance that are cheering for the believers.

One Bible version records Hebrews 12:1-2a this way - We have all these great people around us as examples. Their lives tell us what faith means. So we, too, should run the race that is before us and never quit. *We should remove from our lives anything that would slow us down and the sin that so often makes us fall.* When involved in bodybuilding, you must gradually ADD weight to gain strength and build muscle. However, in Christian bodybuilding, that is not true. The main reason is because "weight" in the Christian walk is equated with "sin." Adding sin to our lives does not strengthen us. We should learn from those encounters, but the sin itself (which is the weight) does not strengthen us. Paul sandwiches the words in our reference passage with this encouragement. We are encouraged during this race by the witness of those who ran before us, and their success was assured because they kept their focus on the creator and the completer of their faith, Jesus Christ.

Although we learn from the examples of others within the faith that ran before us, we too must place our ultimate focus on Jesus. Paul tells us that we must never stop looking to Jesus. He is the leader of our faith, and he is the one who makes our faith complete. Starting and ending with Him is how we prepare for our race. Be blessed and run your race in Jesus Name, Amen.

One Year in Devotional Studies

Daily Devotional Reading

Week 44

- **Monday -** *Proverbs 16:1-3*
- **Tuesday -** *1 Corinthians 9:24*
- **Wednesday -** *St. Mark 10:17*
- **Thursday -** *Exodus 15:2*
- **Friday -** *Joshua 1:11*
- **Saturday -** *2 Samuel 15:1*

One Year in Devotional Studies

Week 45

As "It" Is Written

"My little children, these things write I unto you, that ye sin not. And if any man sin, we have an advocate with the Father, Jesus Christ the righteous: [2] And he is the propitiation for our sins: and not for ours only, but also for the sins of the whole world."

I John 2:1-2

Over the course of my work years I have had a variety of managers. Each of them had their own unique way of managing. One of them had a requirement that every request made had to be put in writing. Many of my co-workers did not like this requirement. All of the past managers would hold monthly meetings where any issues or concerns could be brought, expressed and addressed. Once expressed, the Manager would acknowledge the request and make a declaration to investigate and implement the necessary processes for improvement.

The problem however was that too often, that part of the process never happened. Sometimes the request soon lost its importance and priority. Sometimes it was over-shadowed by another concern introduced at the next meeting, of greater value. Sometimes, what was heard was not exactly what was said. Sometimes office politics got in the way and the concern simply died. I don't think I was the only one but I welcomed the written process because it accomplished several things;

> *"It became a written document of commitment. It was protected from someone later misrepresenting the request. It eventually became an honorable process with a consistent track record. It invoked accountability on both the requester as well as the implementer of change. Lastly and maybe more personally, I liked putting my request in writing."*

The Word of God is a great example of these positives. God says in our theme text at **I John 2:1**, these things write I unto you, that ye sin not. **Romans 8:36** says, As it is written, For thy sake we are killed all the day long; God says to Moses at **Exodus 24:12**, My commandments which I have written; that thou mayest teach them, At **Malachi 3:16** the Prophet recorded, a book of remembrance was written before him for them that feared the Lord, In **Revelation 1:3** we find these words, Blessed is he that readeth, and they that hear the words of this prophecy, and keep those things which are written therein: for the time is at hand. The words write and written are used 357 times in the KJV of the Bible. How important is this?

It is more important than anything in life because your very life depends on it. Our God is immutable, He cannot lie! He is a man of His word. He's so trustworthy and deserving of this honor. So much so, He puts it in writing. When we familiarize ourselves with His word, we build our confidence in our walk because through His word we know we are not walking alone. How do I know this to be true? Because "It Is Written." In Jesus Name, Amen.

One Year in Devotional Studies

Daily Devotional Reading

Week 45

- **Monday -** *Hebrews 13:8*
- **Tuesday -** *Exodus 24:12*
- **Wednesday -** *Deuteronomy 28:58*
- **Thursday -** *Joshua 1:8*
- **Friday -** *Job 19:23*
- **Saturday -** *St. Matthew 4:10*

One Year in Devotional Studies

Week 46

Humbling Ourselves

"Humble yourselves therefore under the mighty hand of God, that he may exalt you in due time:"

I Peter 5:6

Too many people think that being humble is being a doormat. Jesus was the epitome of humility, and there was nothing doormat about Him. I read a catch phrase once on a church billboard that said, "Being humble is not thinking less of yourself, it is thinking of yourself less." I thought that was very appropriate. Paul said at Romans 12:3, "That we are not to think more highly of ourselves than we ought to," but he never said that there was or is anything wrong with thinking highly of ourselves. When we consider the great, High and Lofty God that we serve and that it is He that has us where we are and causes us to be who we are in life, how can we not think highly of ourselves? That is something to hold in high esteem. We are, however, humbled by staying mindful of the reality God sets us up in life.

Let's look at Paul's message in Ephesians 6 verse 12 -

"For we wrestle not against flesh and blood, but against principalities, against powers, against the rulers of the

> *darkness of this world, against spiritual wickedness in high places."*

We must first realize and recognize that we are going to encounter "wrestling" in our walk with Christ. Secondly, wrestling is "spiritual" and it's going to be a "battle." In life, it is tough enough fighting against things that we see, let alone things we can't see. Nevertheless, this is the challenge before us. The good news is that we don't have to take on this challenge alone. Just as God assured Joshua that He would never leave or forsake him, He also assures us of the same. So as we struggle in this wrestling match that will be a "for real" battle, the key is in the revelation that it is a spiritual one. Satan attacks us in our spirit. What does that mean?

He comes at us focusing on the areas of our life that are weak. We may have allowed these areas to become weak spiritually by slacking off in our study and meditation time, or it may be an area in our life that God wants to build up. Paul gives us the solution in verse 11. He says, "Put on the whole Armour of God that ye may be able to stand against the wiles of the devil." The whole armor involves knowing who you are, where your weaknesses are and trusting and relying on God totally to provide the needed strength in those areas to fend off the devil.

Although the whole armor fully equips, it is not the armor that we trust in. It is the one who fits us with It. When we fully submit and surrender unto the Lord through fervent prayer, He not only hears our prayer but also connects with who we become as a result of it. He then becomes compelled to respond and commune with us creating the most intimate relationship imaginable. It is there in His presence that we find total peace, a peace that surpasses all understanding. What a place to be! And we find ourselves there simply because we humbled ourselves under the Mighty hand of God. May God Bless you in Jesus Name, Amen.

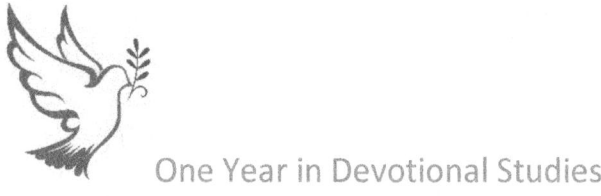
One Year in Devotional Studies

Daily Devotional Reading

Week 46

- **Monday -** *St. James 4:10*
- **Tuesday -** *Exodus 10:3*
- **Wednesday -** *2 Chronicles 7:14*
- **Thursday -** *Psalms 34:2*
- **Friday -** *St. Matthew 18:4*
- **Saturday -** *Philippians 2:8*

One Year in Devotional Studies

Week 47

Using the Strong Name

"Our HELP is in the name of the Lord, Who made Heaven and Earth."

Psalm 124:8

In the Message Bible, this verse says, GOD's strong name is our help, the same GOD who made heaven and earth. We all have strong names. You know names that others use that get a reaction or response from us, such as father, mother, he, she, baby, honey, Pastor, Mr., Sir, ma'am, and other similar positive names. There are also negative names like dummy, silly, loser, and a host of other derogatory terms. Each one yields a different response from the person to whom it is directed. Where one name may produce anger, another may promote compassion.

One of my favorite songs of worship is "If it had not been for the Lord On My Side, where would I be?" I guess that's because I know that is so true when I look back over my life. Even when I made my best decisions, they still paled in comparison to what God has done.

Many years ago I was led to study the various descriptive names of God. As a result, I now have a closer relationship with Him. The song says "If it had not been for the *LORD* on my side." When the name, LORD, is used in scripture and it's in all capital letters, it is translated in the Hebrew as The Unlimited One, Master over the universe, basically, the ONLY One that has total control over every aspect of Life. With a God like that on your side, what else do you need?

Romans 8:31 says, "If God be for us, who can be or who can successfully stand against us? "God is as strong as He will ever be. However, the name that depicts His strength is El Shaddai. Maybe you have a favorite song that has a general name for God in the lyrics. Maybe a song like "How Great Thou Art." Substitute the "Thou" for "El Shaddai," the more enduring manifestation of Almighty God. Watch and see if He is not moved to break that bondage or that stronghold in your life and establish a more intimate relationship with you in the process.

There are a number of special or specific names of our God that many great people of God have used to describe Him. They also used these names to depict their relationship to Him. Either way, when you do this, you are using His Strong names, and you will get the strong results associated with them. Using God's strong name yields strong results and produces a strong Christian life. I pray we all grow to use them more. In Jesus Name, Amen.

One Year in Devotional Studies

Daily Devotional Reading

Week 47

- **Monday -** *Genesis 17:1*
- **Tuesday -** *Ezekiel 10:5*
- **Wednesday -** *Revelation 4:8*
- **Thursday -** *Exodus 17:15*
- **Friday -** *Revelation 11:17*
- **Saturday -** *St. Mark 10:27*

One Year in Devotional Studies

Week 48

For This I Give You Praise

"For great is the LORD, and greatly to be praised: he also is to be feared above all gods. ^{26} For all the gods of the people are idols: but the LORD made the heavens. ^{27} Glory and honour are in his presence; strength and gladness are in his place."
I Chronicles 16:25-27

Life will take us through all kinds of valleys, over mountains of various heights that may seem to be insurmountable and if that's not enough, occasionally, struggles will challenge the very foundation that we rely on for stability and peace of mind. But in all of those diabolical attempts of Satan to destroy us, we are experiencing victory even as we endure these attacks. An accurate view of our struggles will reveal to us that "Jesus is", our Foundation and He has brought us "Through" valleys and "Over" mountains. It may be or may have been very uncomfortable but the truth is, we are stronger because of it. He has never left us nor failed us. And He never will!

Lamentations 3:22-23 says, it is of the Lord's mercies that we are not consumed, because his compassions fail not. They are new every morning: great is thy faithfulness. Paul says at Philippians 4:8, Finally, brethren, whatsoever things are true, whatsoever

Reverend Gregory L. Williamson

things are honest, whatsoever things are just, whatsoever things are pure, whatsoever things are lovely, whatsoever things are of good report; if there be any virtue, and *if there be any praise*, think on these things. I thought about one of my favorite songs of inspiration. If you can, google it, listen to the words and Be Blessed.

I don't know what Kurt Carr was experiencing when he wrote "For Every Mountain" but it will bring perspective and priority back into your life. The lyrics says,

I've got so much to thank God for. So many blessings and so many open doors.
A brand new mercy, Along with each new day
That's why I praise You. For this I give You praise.

For waking me up this morning, For starting me on my way.
For letting me see the sunlight of a brand new day
A brand new mercy along with each new day
That's why I praise You. For this I give You praise.

You're Jehovah Jireh. You've been my provider
So many times You met my need, So many times You rescued me
I wanna thank You for the blessings You give to me each day
That's why I praise You. For this I give You praise.

For every mountain You brought me over. For every trial you've seen me through
For every blessing, Hallelujah, for this I give You praise.

If we think about all of the daily blessings of God that are often overlook, we should say, forgive me Lord for my ingratitude. We should be moved to say, Lord, when I think of your goodness and all you have done for me, my soul cries out, Hallelujah and "For This I Give You Praise." In Jesus Name, Amen.

One Year in Devotional Studies

Daily Devotional Reading

Week 48

- **Monday -** Psalms 150
- **Tuesday -** Judges 5:3
- **Wednesday -** 1 Corinthians 4:5
- **Thursday -** Philippians 4:8
- **Friday -** 2 Chronicles 20:22
- **Saturday -** Psalms 9:1

One Year in Devotional Studies

Week 49

How Good Is Your Memory?

"And forgive us our debts, as we forgive our debtors."
St. Matthew 6:12

If asked, all of us can recall a time in the past when someone offended us or brought some unmerited injustice against us. For some, it may have occurred just a short while ago. For others, it might have been years or decades ago. Unfortunately for so many, the story is told as though it was just yesterday. The pain that was felt in that experience was very real. Equally unwarranted was the injustice associated with it. Nevertheless, it continues to yield the same troubling and puzzling effect it did when it originally occurred.

There are a number of positive reasons to develop a good memory. Appointments, schedules for taking medicine, answers for testing in school, etc. are all good reasons to discipline our minds. There are, however, some negative consequences we experience when we work at memorizing events that we would be better off forgetting. Forgiving is often difficult and forgetting is even more challenging. Nevertheless, for the believer, it is imperative.

Jesus said at Matthew 6:12 - **And forgive us our debts, as we forgive our debtors** or forgive us our trespasses and we forgive those that trespass against us or more simply put, forgive our sins as we forgive others of theirs. The message Jesus is conveying is not that we will lose our salvation if we fail to forgive others when they offend us. Once we truly receive salvation, it is safe and secure in Christ (John 10:27-29). Most importantly, God wants to develop a relationship with us and create an attitude within us that reflects His nature to the world and other believers (Matthew 5:13 and 14).

God reminds us at Isaiah 43:25 that *"I, even I, am He that blotteth out thy transgressions for mine own sake, and will not remember thy sins."* Since God forgives and forgets our sins, and He could legitimately remember them, we should strive to forgive and forget the offenses of others against us. If we consider our transgressions against God and what He sacrificed for us, we should be moved to forgive. Failing to forgive stunts our growth and maturity. If it lingers long enough, it causes others to avoid us. A spiritually disciplined mind discerns what's best remembered and what is best forgotten. Lastly and most importantly, failing to forgive creates a barrier in our communication with God. My prayer today – let Grace dominate, forgive others and forgive yourself. God does! In Jesus Name, Amen.

One Year in Devotional Studies

Daily Devotional Reading

Week 49

- **Monday -** *Ecclesiastes 12:1*
- **Tuesday -** *2 Kings 20:3*
- **Wednesday -** *Micah 6:5*
- **Thursday -** *St. Luke 16:25*
- **Friday -** *1 Corinthians 11:2*
- **Saturday -** *Proverbs 10:7*

One Year in Devotional Studies

Week 50

Where Are You?

"And the LORD *God called unto Adam, and said unto him, Where art thou?"*

Genesis 3:9

If you are reading this message, you are more blessed than you may realize. Not because you are reading "this" message but because you still have both breath and the mental capacity to read. It's 2015 and unlike so many, you are still here. God has shown favor and declared continued purpose for your life. In light of that, I ask the question – "where are you?" Throughout the year, most of us, if not all of us, made commitments and declarations that we intended to keep only to realize here at the inception of a New Year that we didn't "get-ur-done!" Does that mean that the past year was a failure? Does that mean that we were a failure? The answer to both is NO!

Sometimes our best intentions are just that, *"Our"* best intentions, but not God's will for our life in that timeframe. Sometimes we make decisions based on insufficient information. Sometimes we make decisions based on our expected outcome. Sometimes we just shoot from the hip hoping to hit the desired target. In all of these situations, God is moving and causing His desired outcome because He knows not only what is best for the moment but also what's best for the overall outcome. He will always use every situation to bring Him Glory, even when we fail to see it.

When Jesus told Peter that he would deny Him, Peter responded based on his mindset and attitude at the time. He had no idea what he was about to encounter or how troubling and challenging it would be to maintain his present level of commitment and loyalty to Jesus Christ. In the Garden, after man disobeyed God's command not to eat from the forbidden tree, God called out to Adam and asked, "Where are you?" Adam's response was not – "God I messed up. I was disobedient. Would you please forgive me?" Instead he said – "I heard your voice, I was afraid because I was naked, so I hid."

Every day, believers in Christ make decisions, and most often they are honorable ones that we believe will bring about an improvement, maybe for us, maybe for someone else, but an improvement. However, all too often it doesn't work out that way. We then become disappointed, hurt, or confused, blame something else, or move into denial. Our all-knowing (Omniscient) God not only knows what we are doing and what we have done at all times: He also knows how to turn a bad result into a good outcome. However, we must be open with Him and agree to see our actions as He sees them. That's when He can and will apply the Romans 8:28 command. Every experience we encounter is a building block of opportunity for our betterment.

The fact that you are reading this message says that you are more blessed than you may realize. God does not do anything just for the sake of doing it. The fact that you are alive in this New Year says that God has plans for your life that includes this year. So here we are at the beginning of it. What are you going to do with it? Where are you – mentally, spiritually, emotionally, economically? Peter was strengthened by his setback, and we grow and benefit from his epistles even today. Adam and Eve were forgiven, and the

One Year in Devotional Studies

sacrifice of Jesus Christ atoned for their sins as well as ours. We are forgiven as well. Whatever did or didn't happen in the last year, let it go. It's behind you now. Let's collectively move forward. Focus on what God has for you in the New Year. Let's complete that assignment. As Apostle Paul said at Phil. 3:14 - *I press toward the mark for the prize of the high calling of God in Christ Jesus.* Have a Happy New Year. All 365 days of it. Be Blessed in Jesus Name, Amen.

Daily Devotional Reading

Week 50

- **Monday -** Genesis 3:9
- **Tuesday -** St. Luke 15:6
- **Wednesday -** Jeremiah 50:6
- **Thursday -** St. Matthew 15:24
- **Friday -** Ezekiel 34:4
- **Saturday -** St. Luke 9:25

One Year in Devotional Studies

Week 51

They Found Him

"And it came to pass, that after three days they found him in the temple, sitting in the midst of the doctors, both hearing them, and asking them questions."

St. Luke 2:46

This time of year is always a very busy and challenging time. It can also be very stressful for some. In some instances, the fulfillment of children's Christmas wishes and/or the expectations of friends, family and acquaintances can produce pressure and discomfort. For some of us, we find ourselves reminiscing about family members or friends that are no longer with us physically. That can be emotionally draining. In reality, this season is really all about Jesus and what He has provided us through His birth, death and resurrection.

In the text above, we find the announcement of Jesus' birth, who He is and what His birth means to the world. We see where His focus was, even from His youth. While returning from the Feast in Jerusalem, Mary and Joseph discover that Jesus is not with them. The passage goes on to say, "After three days they found Him."

Many people spend this time catching up on things that need attention, such as relationships that have suffered, been shattered or fractured but there never seemed enough time to appropriately address them. I encourage you to focus on the important things in life, things that really matter: relationships! Gifts are great, but they are temporary.

The passage above tells us that "After Three Days, They Found Him." This implies that they lost Him. That might seem hard to believe, but it is not uncommon or impossible to lose Jesus. Sometimes through the hustle and bustle of life, we lose Him. What I mean by lose Him is "We lose our focus on Him." What is most important is that we not become comfortable in that state. We need to find Him. Joseph and Mary found Him. It took them three days, but they found Him.

It might not always take three days. It could be three weeks, three years or three seconds. The most important factor here is to "Find Him." If you know Him, be thankful for the relationship you have in Christ during this season, but be prayerful that others will seek and find Him as well. Finding Jesus and developing a relationship with Him are not just what this season is all about; it's what life is all about. Be Blessed and enjoy your Christmas Season. In Jesus Name, Amen.

One Year in Devotional Studies

Daily Devotional Reading

Week 51

- **Monday -** *St. Mark 11:4-8*
- **Tuesday -** *Genesis 6:8*
- **Wednesday -** *Exodus 33:17*
- **Thursday -** *Philippians 2:8*
- **Friday -** *Genesis 18:32*
- **Saturday -** *2 Peter 3:14*

One Year in Devotional Studies

Week 52

Looking for Opportunities

⁹ "And let us not be weary in well doing: for in due season we shall reap, if we faint not. ¹⁰ As we have therefore opportunity, let us do good unto all men, especially unto them who are of the household of faith."

Galatians 6:9-10

The military uses a slogan for recruiting in the Marine division that says – "We are looking for a few good men." In the Bible, Jesus says at Matthew 9:37, "Then saith he unto his disciples, The harvest truly is plenteous, but the labourers are few." Simply put, there was a great need for committed workers in Jesus' day, and there remains a great need even today for people that are willing to help in time of need.

My wife blessed me with a birthday trip to the Dominican Republic, and among all of the beauty and bliss that I experienced, I also realized the advantage of American money there. A little bit truly goes a long way. The residents of Punta Cana would do almost anything to make sure you were comfortable and satisfied, all for a crisp "one dollar bill." The amount of food choices 24/7 was unbelievable. As I looked around the dining areas of each restaurant, I noticed enormous amounts of food being continuously discarded. I thought about the various TV ministries I've seen displaying starving children across our land that don't have sufficient amounts or choices of food to eat.

When we returned to Michigan, we looked forward to spending time during the Christmas holiday season with our family and friends. We prayed as we always do for those less fortunate, those experiencing challenges like bereavement or illness during this season, and for the opportunity to make a difference where we could. While in route to my sister's home for family dinner, we stopped to dispose of some trash, and to our surprise, we saw a man maybe in his late 50s or early 60s raking through the dumpsters. He had gathered several discarded containers of partially eaten food that he was setting aside, I presumed to later eat. I spoke to the man, dumped the trash and we drove off. As we drove off it wasn't more than a few minutes before I remembered our prayer – *Lord give us opportunity to make a difference*. We turned around and went back. He was still there. We just gave him money, wished him a Merry Christmas and left. He just stared at me and said, thank you.

Whether large or small, we all have something that we can offer to make life a little brighter for those we see from day to day. We can't afford to grow weary in doing well. So many people are depending on us. God's reward, both now and in heaven, is awaiting us, and it's more than worth the labor. So I ask again, *Are You Looking for Opportunities?* Be a blessing. In Jesus Name, Amen.

One Year in Devotional Studies

Daily Devotional Reading

Week 52

- **Monday -** Acts 25:16
- **Tuesday -** 1 Timothy 5:14
- **Wednesday -** Romans 7:8
- **Thursday -** St. Luke 21:13
- **Friday -** Galatians 5:13
- **Saturday -** 1 Samuel 10:7

www.ingramcontent.com/pod-product-compliance
Lightning Source LLC
LaVergne TN
LVHW052100090426
835512LV00036B/2742